QUICK & EASY

QUICK & EASY

SIMPLE, EVERYDAY RECIPES
IN 30 MINUTES OR LESS

Project Editor Siobhán O'Connor
Project Designer Alison Shackleton
Editors Kiron Gill, Megan Lea
US Editors Jenny Wilson, Lori Hand
US Consultant Renee Wilmeth
Jacket Designer Alison Donovan
Jackets Coordinator Jasmin Lennie
Production Editor David Almond
Production Controller Denitsa Kenanska
Managing Editor Dawn Henderson
Managing Art Editor Alison Donovan
Art Director Maxine Pedliham
Publishing Director Katie Cowan

First American Edition, 2022
Published in the United States by DK Publishing
1450 Broadway, Suite 801, New York, NY 10018

Copyright © 2022 Dorling Kindersley Limited
DK, a Division of Penguin Random House LLC
22 23 24 25 26 10 9 8 7 6 5 4 3 2 1
001–326302–Mar/2022

A catalog record for this book is available from the Library of Congress.
ISBN 978-0-7440-5036-3

DK books are available at special discounts when purchased in bulk
for sales promotions, premiums, fund-raising, or educational use.
For details, contact: DK Publishing Special Markets, 1450 Broadway,
Suite 800, New York, NY 10018 SpecialSales@dk.com

Printed and bound in China

For the curious
www.dk.com

This book was made with Forest Stewardship Council™ certified paper—
one small step in DK's commitment to a sustainable future.
For more information go to **www.dk.com/our-green-pledge**.

Contents

Quick and Easy

**Food for the modern cook—home cooking where convenience is key.
Our modern lives are jam-packed with distractions, whether that be work,
family, the gym, or just finding the time to do a load of washing. With all these
conflicting obligations, one of the first things sacrificed is your time in the
kitchen and a home-cooked dinner.**

Cooking doesn't need to be hard or time-consuming. Our recipes have been developed with the modern cook in mind, using simple or prepackaged ingredients and ingenious cooking tricks to get your dinner on the table in no time at all.

As we have all become more health-conscious and food-savvy, supermarkets have responded to our concerns with an array of good-quality ready-made products that make all the difference when trying to prepare dinner quickly. Embrace the premade sauce, the microwaveable grains, the marinated and diced meats, and don't be afraid to purchase something (of good quality) to speed up the cooking process. What is important here is you in the kitchen. Find the joy in being able to make delicious and healthy homemade food, and never rely on takeout again. All our recipes feature one of the following labels to help guide your meal choices. Also, remember to take advantage of the tips and tricks on the opposite page.

CHEAP EAT
A bargain dinner In-season, readily available fresh ingredients are great for budget-conscious cooks.

HEALTHY CHOICE
Better for you This takes all the guesswork out of trying to find fast, healthy food choices.

MEAT-FREE
Veggie meal option Not just for Mondays—meat-free is a great way to start eating more fresh vegetables.

ONE-PAN
Quick clean-up Great for those nights you can't be bothered with multiple pots, pans, and doing dishes.

GLUTEN-FREE
Celiac's choice In recipes labelled 'GLUTEN-FREE', all ingredients are safe for those who cannot eat gluten.

DAIRY-FREE
No hidden dairy No dairy products are used—but, if using prepackaged food, read the label carefully.

KID-FRIENDLY
Great for kids Meals with children in mind—not so spicy, not too much cilantro, but still full of flavor.

PREP STEPS

1 Quick herbs

To quickly chop soft-leaf herbs (such as flat-leaf parsley, cilantro, and dill), use your hands to twist off the stems from the bunch in one go, then chop the leaves and edible stems together.

2 Great grate

To grate vegetables such as carrots and zucchini quickly, use the shredder attachment on a food processor; for cabbage, use the slicer attachment.

3 Acidulated water

This is simply water with lemon juice added. Use it to prevent fennel, apple, and pears from turning brown. Avocado, however, can be stored cut-side down, with the skin on, in plain water to stop it from browning.

4 More juice

For speed and to maximize the amount of juice extracted from lemons and limes, first roll the fruit firmly on a hard bench or work surface using the palm of your hand, or microwave on HIGH (100%) for 15 seconds, before juicing.

5 Herb-ready

Freeze fresh herbs such as thyme, rosemary, and chives, either chopped or in whole-leaf form, in measured quantities in ice-cube trays and covered with a thin layer of olive oil. Simply add the herbs to your recipe straight from the freezer, increasing convenience and cutting down on food wastage.

6 Marinating

To make marinating easier, put the marinating ingredients and the meat or fish in a large zip-top plastic bag; seal the bag and massage the marinade into the ingredients. Leave it in the fridge for at least 3 hours or overnight.

7 Fishy tales

If you aren't a fan of fish skin, there's no need to fuss about trying to remove it before cooking—leave it on, as the skin will hold the delicate flesh of the fish together while it cooks. Peel away the skin when the fish is done; it should lift away easily.

8 Do-ahead

Start the recipe the morning or day before. Measure out the ingredients and store the perishable ones in the fridge. Hard vegetables, with the exception of potatoes, can be cut on the morning of cooking; store covered with damp paper towels.

9 Quick clean

For easy cleaning, and to prevent ingredients from sticking, line the bottom of the pan and halfway up the sides with parchment paper. Cook as instructed, then discard the parchment when finished.

EXPRESS LUNCHES

Need speedy remedies for what to make for a lunchtime snack or a casual meal with family or friends, or even what to pack for work or the school lunch box? This is the place to go.

Green turkey wraps

GLUTEN-FREE | PREP + COOK TIME **30 MINUTES** | SERVES **4**

Lettuce takes the place of bread in these crunchy wraps. Transport the filled lettuce wraps and green tahini sauce packed separately, to prevent the wraps from becoming soggy, then drizzle with the sauce, roll up to make the wraps, and enjoy.

1 tbsp extra virgin olive oil

½ lb (225g) sweet potatoes, cut into ¼ in rounds

1 avocado (150g)

1 tbsp lemon juice

½ lb (225g) shaved deli turkey breast

2 small tomatoes (180g), thinly sliced

¼ cup (70g) julienned carrot

1 cucumber (130g), julienned

¼ cup (50g) thinly sliced red onion

12 romaine lettuce leaves (see tip)

green tahini sauce

¼ cup (70g) tahini

2 tbsp flat-leaf parsley leaves

2 tbsp lemon juice

1 tbsp extra virgin olive oil

1 small garlic clove, crushed

salt and freshly ground black pepper

1 To make the green tahini sauce, place the ingredients in a jar with a tightly-fitting screw top. Shake well to combine. Add salt and pepper to taste. Add a little water if the mixture is too thick. Set aside.

2 Heat the olive oil in a large nonstick sauté pan over low heat. Cook the sweet potato, turning, for 8 minutes or until tender.

3 Slice the avocado in half. Remove the pit. Thinly slice the avocado inside of the skin, then carefully remove the slices with a spoon. Put the slices in a small bowl, toss with the lemon juice, then drain.

4 Divide the avocado, sweet potato, shaved turkey, tomatoes, carrot, cucumber, and onion evenly among each of the lettuce leaves. Just before serving, drizzle with the green tahini dressing and fold the lettuce around the fillings to enclose.

TIP

Try romaine hearts instead of full heads for leaves that are a good size for this dish.

Shrimp cocktail sandwiches with fries

KID-FRIENDLY | PREP + COOK TIME **30 MINUTES** | SERVES **4**

In a classic combination, sweet, juicy shrimp and tangy cocktail sauce bring summer to your plate. As usual with a simple dish, it's best to choose good-quality ingredients so that they shine. Also, make sure to choose the most flavorful ripe tomatoes you can find.

1³/₄ lbs (800g) frozen French fries

2 tsp olive oil

4 slices of thick-cut bacon (100g), each cut into three pieces

¹/₂ cup (150g) mayonnaise

2 tsp ketchup

a few drops of hot sauce

8 slices of white sourdough bread (560g)

1 small head of butter lettuce, leaves separated

2 tomatoes (300g), thinly sliced

1 lb (500g) shelled, cooked shrimp

sea salt flakes

1   Preheat the oven to 425°F. Line a baking sheet with parchment paper.

2   Arrange the fries in a single layer on the baking sheet. Season with sea salt to taste. Cook in the oven according to the package directions.

3   Meanwhile, heat the olive oil in a large sauté pan over high heat; cook the bacon until crisp. Drain on paper towels.

4   Combine the mayonnaise, ketchup, and hot sauce to taste in a small bowl. Spread the bread with the mayonnaise mixture. Sandwich the lettuce, bacon, sliced tomato, and shrimp between the bread slices. Serve with the hot fries.

TIP

You can use fresh shrimp if you like. Simply use 2 lbs of shrimp, steam in the shells, then peel and devein.

Grilled veggies and squash dip wraps

GLUTEN-FREE | PREP + COOK TIME **10 MINUTES** | MAKES **4**

These wraps can also be quickly assembled at work for a portable lunch; pack all the ingredients in separate containers, and assemble when you're ready to eat. Not only does this help to avoid soggy wraps, but it keeps the peppery crunch in the arugula as well.

2 x 10 oz jars mixed grilled vegetables packed in oil

8 oz (225g) Moroccan butternut squash dip

4 x 8 in gluten-free tortillas

2 cups (40g) arugula leaves

salt and freshly ground black pepper

1 Drain the grilled vegetables and dry on paper towels. Season with salt and pepper to taste.

2 Spread the dip onto the wraps; top with the chargrilled vegetables and arugula. Roll up to enclose the fillings.

TIPS

- You can substitute the butternut squash dip for roasted red pepper hummus or baba ghanoush.
- Use your favorite brand of gluten-free rolls instead of tortillas, if you like.
- Make sure to pat the grilled vegetables dry with paper towels; otherwise the wraps will be soggy by lunchtime if made ahead.

Tuna and olive baguettes

CHEAP EAT | PREP + COOK TIME **10 MINUTES** | MAKES **4**

The complementary pairing of tuna and salty olives used in these baguette sandwiches is one found across the Mediterranean. You could also use a chili- or lemon-flavored tuna for the filling. For an even more hunger-satisfying sandwich, add 2 sliced hard-boiled eggs.

2 x 12 in baguettes

$^1/_3$ cup (80g) mayonnaise

3 x 5.4 oz (459g) cans tuna in oil, drained

$^1/_3$ cup (50g) pitted kalamata olives, sliced

1 large tomato (220g), thickly sliced

$^1/_4$ cup (80g) thinly sliced red onion

1 cucumber (130g), cut into ribbons

2 tbsp micro basil leaves

1 Split open the baguettes without cutting all the way through. Spread the cut sides of the bread with mayonnaise.

2 Sandwich the tuna, olives, tomato, onion, cucumber, and basil leaves between the baguette halves.

3 Cut each baguette in half. Serve cut into smaller pieces, if you like.

TIP

Use your favorite gluten-free bread or wraps, instead of baguettes, if you like.

Veggie and chickpea fritters

MEAT-FREE | PREP + COOK TIME **30 MINUTES** | SERVES **4**

Fritters are a great way to incorporate vegetables into the diet of fussy eaters, and are delicious eaten warm or cold. While we've used mint in the recipe here, any soft-leaf herb such as basil, cilantro, or flat-leaf parsley will work well.

1 x 15 oz (425g) can chickpeas, drained, rinsed

³/₄ cup (110g) whole-wheat flour

¹/₂ cup (125ml) milk

2 eggs

³/₄ cup (120g) frozen corn and peas

1 roasted red pepper in oil, drained, finely chopped

2 green onions, thinly sliced

1 small zucchini (90g), coarsely grated

1 small carrot (70g), coarsely grated

¹/₂ cup (60g) coarsely grated cheddar cheese

2 tbsp coarsely chopped mint leaves

2 tbsp extra virgin olive oil

salt and freshly ground black pepper

1 Blend or process the chickpeas until coarsely chopped.

2 Sift the flour into a medium bowl. Lightly whisk together the milk and eggs in a separate, small bowl. Make a well in the center of the flour; stir in the combined milk-and-egg mixture until smooth. Stir in the chickpeas, peas and mixed vegetables, red pepper, green onions, zucchini, carrot, cheddar cheese, and mint. Season with alt and pepper to taste.

3 Heat the olive oil in a large nonstick pan over medium heat. Once the oil is hot, drop ¹/₄ cup (60ml) batter for each fritter, in batches, into the pan (allow room for the mixture to spread). Cook for 3 minutes, then carefully flip over. Cook until the fritters are lightly browned on both sides and cooked through.

TIP

Serve the fritters with a spicy tomato ketchup and mixed salad leaves, if you like.

Bell pepper and ricotta frittata

MEAT-FREE | PREP + COOK TIME **30 MINUTES** | SERVES **6**

The frittata can be eaten hot, warm, or at room temperature, making it ideal for a relaxed lunch, an outdoor picnic, or even a portable lunchtime choice for work. Or do as the Spanish do and serve any leftover frittata stuffed into rolls with ham and other sandwich trappings.

8 eggs

$1/4$ cup (60ml) milk

$1/3$ cup (40g) coarsely grated cheddar cheese

1 tbsp extra virgin olive oil

$1/4$ cup (7g) fresh basil

$1/2$ cup (100g) ricotta cheese

1 red bell pepper (200g), seeded, thinly sliced

1 green bell pepper (200g), seeded, thinly sliced

salt and freshly ground black pepper

1 Preheat the oven to 425°F.

2 In a large bowl, whisk together the eggs, milk, and cheddar cheese; season with salt and pepper to taste.

3 Heat the olive oil in an 8 inch ovenproof skillet over medium heat. Add the egg mixture to the pan; cook for 3 minutes, scraping the edges of the egg into the center of the pan. Top with the basil, chunks of the ricotta cheese, and bell peppers. Cook the frittata, without stirring, over medium heat for 2 minutes or until the bottom and edges are almost set. Transfer the pan to the oven. Bake for 15 minutes or until set and lightly browned. Allow to stand in the pan for 5 minutes.

4 Slide the frittata onto a serving plate, and cut into wedges to serve.

TIP

You will need a skillet with an ovenproof handle for this recipe, or cover the handle with a few layers of foil to protect it from the heat of the oven.

Creamy chicken and pasta salad

CHEAP EAT | PREP + COOK TIME **30 MINUTES** | SERVES **6**

Whether you're a big kid or a little kid, this refreshing but filling salad would also make a great supper. Double the recipe and not only do you have a simple evening meal at the end of a busy day, but lunch for work the next day is covered as well.

³/₄ lb (400g) skinless boneless chicken breasts

¹/₂ lb (500g) large dried pasta shells

3 celery sticks (300g), trimmed, thinly sliced

¹/₂ cup (150g) thinly sliced red onion

1 cup (120g) roasted pecans

¹/₂ cup (90g) thinly sliced dill pickles

2¹/₂ cups (50g) arugula

salt and freshly ground black pepper

creamy tarragon dressing

³/₄ cup (225g) mayonnaise

¹/₂ cup (120g) sour cream

2 tbsp lemon juice

1 tbsp finely chopped tarragon

1 Bring 3 cups (750ml) water to a boil in a medium saucepan. Add the whole chicken breasts; simmer, covered, for 10 minutes. Allow the chicken to cool in the poaching liquid for 10 minutes, then drain. Coarsely shred into large, bite-sized pieces.

2 Meanwhile, cook the pasta in a large saucepan of boiling salted water according to the package directions until almost tender; drain. Rinse under cold running water; drain again.

3 To make the creamy tarragon dressing, combine the ingredients in a small bowl and mix through evenly.

4 Put the pasta in a large bowl with the shredded chicken, tarragon dressing, and the remaining ingredients. Gently toss through. Season with salt and pepper to taste.

TIPS

• Use cornichons or other small gherkins in place of the dill pickles, if you like.

• If you would prefer a vinaigrette dressing, put ¹/₄ cup (60ml) olive oil, ¹/₄ cup (60ml) lemon juice, and the finely chopped tarragon in a screw-top jar with a tight-fitting lid; shake well to combine.

Teriyaki chicken rice paper rolls

KID-FRIENDLY/CHEAP EAT | PREP + COOK TIME **30 MINUTES** | MAKES **24**

The trick to assembling Vietnamese-style fresh rice paper rolls is to soak the rice paper wrappers until only just softened. Once they are removed from the water, the wrappers will continue to soften, making them pliable enough to fold easily.

1½ lb (660g) boneless chicken thighs

¼ cup (60ml) teriyaki sauce

4 cucumbers (520g)

8 oz (225g) enoki mushrooms

2 tsp peanut oil

24 x 8-in square rice paper wrappers

lime and sweet chili dipping sauce

⅓ cup (80ml) sweet chili sauce

2 tbsp lime juice

1 Trim the chicken and cut each fillet into 4 strips lengthwise. Combine the chicken and marinade in a small bowl. Set aside.

2 Meanwhile, cut the cucumbers in half lengthwise; scoop out the seeds. Cut the cucumber halves in half crosswise; cut the pieces into 3 strips lengthwise. Trim the enoki mushrooms.

3 Drain the chicken; discard the marinade. Heat the oil in a large sauté pan over medium-high heat; cook the chicken, in batches, for 3 minutes or until cooked through. Allow to cool for 10 minutes.

4 Meanwhile, to make the lime and sweet chili dipping sauce, combine the ingredients in a small bowl.

5 Once the chicken has cooled, place 1 rice paper wrapper in a medium bowl of warm water until just softened. Carefully lift the wrapper from the water and place on a cutting board covered with a clean kitchen towel. Place 2 pieces of the chicken horizontally in the center of the rice paper wrapper; top with 2 pieces of the cucumber, then a few mushrooms. Fold the side nearest you over the filling; roll up the rice paper wrapper to enclose the filling, folding in one side after the first complete turn of roll. Repeat with the remaining rice paper wrappers, chicken, cucumber, and mushrooms. Serve the rice paper rolls with the dipping sauce.

TIP

Keep the rice paper rolls fresh by covering them with a slightly damp piece of paper towel, then store them in an airtight container in the refrigerator.

Tuna and quinoa niçoise salad

HEALTHY CHOICE | PREP + COOK TIME **30 MINUTES** | SERVES **4**

Quinoa makes an appearance here alongside the more traditional salade niçoise ingredients of tomatoes, eggs, olives, and tuna. This lunch salad can be prepared the night before for an office lunch. Pack the salad and vinaigrette separately, and combine just before serving.

1½ cups (300g) red quinoa

4 eggs, at room temperature (see tips)

½ lb (225g) green beans, trimmed

3 x 5.4 oz (459g) can tuna in oil, drained, flaked

8 oz (250g) cherry tomatoes, halved

½ cup (60g) pitted kalamata olives

½ cup (15g) firmly packed flat-leaf parsley leaves

1 tbsp finely chopped chives

caper and parmesan cheese vinaigrette

1 tbsp drained capers, rinsed, chopped

¼ cup (20g) finely grated Parmesan cheese

¼ cup (60ml) white wine vinegar

2 tbsp extra virgin olive oil

1 small garlic clove, crushed

1 tsp Dijon mustard

1 tsp sugar

sea salt and freshly ground black pepper

1 Cook the quinoa in a large saucepan of boiling water for 12 minutes or until tender; drain. Set aside to cool.

2 Meanwhile, cook the eggs in a small saucepan of boiling water for 6 minutes until medium-boiled. Drain, then cool the eggs under cold running water. Peel carefully, then halve the eggs. Set aside.

3 Boil, steam, or microwave the green beans until tender; drain. Rinse under cold water to refresh; drain.

4 Meanwhile, to make the caper and parmesan cheese vinaigrette, combine the ingredients in a small bowl; season with sea salt and pepper to taste.

5 Put the quinoa and beans in a large bowl with the tuna, cherry tomatoes, olives, parsley, and vinaigrette; toss to combine. Serve the quinoa salad topped with the egg halves and the chives sprinkled over the top.

TIP

If you forget to bring the eggs to room temperature first, place them straight from the fridge into a saucepan of cold water; bring to a boil, then boil for 5 minutes. If you want to "center" the egg yolks, gently stir the eggs until the water comes to a boil.

Toasted phyllo empanadas

KID-FRIENDLY | PREP + COOK TIME **30 MINUTES** | MAKES **6**

These classic South American treats are made easy using phyllo dough and a sandwich press. They're perfect for lunch boxes or quick weeknight suppers. You can even change the filling, substituting the same amount of ground chicken or firm tofu for the ground beef.

1 egg

1/3 cup (80ml) olive oil, divided

1/2 cup (80g) finely chopped onion

2 garlic cloves, crushed

1/2 tsp sweet paprika

1/2 tsp ground coriander

1/2 tsp ground cumin

1/2 tsp dried oregano

1/2 lb (225g) lean ground beef

1/2 cup (60g) chopped tomato

1/3 cup (50g) pimento-stuffed green olives, finely chopped

12 sheets phyllo pastry, thawed

1 cup (120g) grated cheddar cheese

salt and freshly ground black pepper

2 tbsp coriander, to serve (optional)

adobo mayonnaise

1/2 cup (150g) mayonnaise

1 tbsp chipotle chili paste

1 Cook the egg in a saucepan of boiling water for 9 minutes or until hard boiled; cool. Peel and coarsely chop. Set aside.

2 Heat 1 tablespoon of the oil in a skillet over high heat. Add the onion; cook, stirring, for 2 minutes. Add the garlic, paprika, coriander, cumin, and oregano; cook for a further 1 minute until fragrant. Add the ground beef; cook, stirring to break up any lumps, for 3 minutes or until browned and cooked through. Add the tomato; cook, stirring, for 2 minutes or until any liquid is evaporated.

3 Remove the pan from the heat; stir through the chopped egg and olives. Season with salt and pepper to taste; cool slightly to prevent the pastry from becoming soggy when you assemble the empanadas.

4 To make the adobo mayonnaise, stir the ingredients together in a small bowl until combined.

5 On a clean work surface, layer 2 rectangular sheets of the phyllo pastry, brushing each sheet with a little of the olive oil. Place 1/4 cup of the beef mixture and 2 tablespoons of the cheese in a corner of the pastry sheet. Fold the opposite corner of pastry across the filling to form a triangle; fold any excess pastry over and tuck under the triangle. Repeat with the remaining pastry, olive oil, beef mixture, and cheese to make a total of 6 triangles.

6 Preheat a sandwich press. Brush each triangle with a little of the olive oil; cook in the hot sandwich press for 7 minutes until golden and crisp.

7 Cut the empanadas in half, and serve with the adobo mayonnaise and cilantro leaves sprinkled over the top, if you like.

TIP

These empanadas can be cooked to the end of step 6 the night before. You can also freeze them for up to 1 month; thaw in the fridge.

Sweet chili chicken and BLAT salad

CHEAP EAT | PREP + COOK TIME **25 MINUTES** | SERVES **4**

We've taken the flavors of our favorite lunchtime sandwich and reinvented it as
a substantial salad. If you don't want to forego bread, then simply serve the salad with
sourdough and add lemon wedges for squeezing over to add freshness.

4 skinless boneless chicken breasts, about 1¾ lb (800g)

2 tbsp extra virgin olive oil

¼ cup (125ml) sweet chili sauce

1 garlic clove, crushed

⅓ cup (80ml) lime juice

8 slices thick-cut bacon, about ½ lb (225g)

8 oz (225g) cherry vine tomatoes

⅓ cup (100g) mayonnaise

1 tbsp finely chopped flat-leaf parsley

2 romaine hearts (100g), leaves separated

2 avocados (300g), thinly sliced lengthwise

salt and freshly ground black pepper

1 Preheat a ridged cast-iron grill pan over medium heat.

2 Combine the chicken, olive oil, sweet chili sauce, garlic, and half of the lime juice in a medium bowl; season with salt and pepper to taste. Cook the chicken, in batches, on the grill pan for 5 minutes on each side or until cooked through and grill marks appear. Remove from the heat, cover, and set aside to keep warm.

3 Meanwhile, cook the bacon and tomatoes in a sauté pan over medium heat until the bacon is crisp and the tomatoes begin to soften.

4 Combine the mayonnaise, remaining lime juice, and parsley in a small bowl; stir to mix through evenly.

5 Arrange the lettuce on 4 serving plates; top with the chicken, bacon, tomatoes, and avocado; drizzle with the dressing. Serve immediately.

TIP

The number-one mistake people make when grilling is being impatient. Allow the chicken enough time before turning it over that it develops char marks and doesn't stick to the grill.

Corn and quinoa chowder

MEAT-FREE | PREP + COOK TIME **30 MINUTES** | SERVES **4**

This contemporary take on corn chowder omits added starch for thickening and instead relies on quinoa to do the job. If you seek out a gluten-free stock and gluten-free tortillas, this recipe is also suitable for celiac diets.

2 tbsp olive oil

4 ears of corn, husks and silk removed

³/₄ cup (200g), finely chopped onion

1 large russet potato (300g), peeled, coarsely chopped

2 garlic cloves, crushed

1 tsp smoked paprika

4 cups (1 liter) vegetable stock

¹/₂ cup (125ml) heavy cream

¹/₃ cup (70g) red or white quinoa

³/₄ cup (180ml) water

¹/₃ cup (7g) loosely packed cilantro leaves

4 x 8-in whole-grain tortillas, toasted, torn

2 limes (130g), halved

salt and freshly ground black pepper

guacamole

2 avocados (300g), coarsely mashed

1 green onion, thinly sliced

2 tbsp lime juice

1   Heat a large pot of water to boiling. Add the corn and cook for 15 minutes. Remove and let cool. Trim the kernels of the cob.

2   Heat the oil in a large saucepan over medium heat; cook the corn, onion, and potato, covered, for 8 minutes until the onion softens. Add the garlic and half of the paprika; cook, stirring, for 1 minute until fragrant.

3   Add the stock and cream; bring to a boil over high heat. Reduce the heat to medium; cook, covered, for 10 minutes or until the potato is tender. Remove from the heat; allow to stand for 5 minutes. Blend or process half of the chowder until almost smooth; return to the pan. Season with salt and pepper to taste. Stir over the heat until hot.

4   Meanwhile, put the quinoa and ³/₄ cup (180ml) water in a small saucepan; bring to a boil. Reduce the heat to low; cook, covered, for 12 minutes until tender. Allow the quinoa to stand, covered, for 10 minutes, then fluff with a fork. Stir the quinoa through the chowder.

5   Meanwhile, in a separate bowl, make the guacamole. Combine the avocado, green onion, and lime juice in a small bowl; season with salt and pepper to taste.

6   Ladle the chowder into 4 serving bowls; top with the guacamole, cilantro leaves, and remaining paprika. Serve with the tortillas and lime halves for squeezing over.

TIP

Use an immersion blender directly in the soup to blend it while hot. Otherwise, let it cool before adding to a blender or food processor.

Chicken, asparagus, and kale Caesar salad

KID-FRIENDLY | PREP + COOK TIME **30 MINUTES** | SERVES **4**

Classic Caesar salad gets an update with chicken and kale, and green goddess dressing in place of the usual anchovy mayonnaise. The trick to using kale in a salad is to massage the leaves for a few minutes first, either with a little oil and salt, or in the dressing on its own.

12 thin slices of sourdough baguette (100g)

¾ cup (80g) finely grated Parmesan cheese

1 tbsp extra virgin olive oil

8 prosciutto slices (120g)

¾ lb (300g) fresh asparagus, trimmed, halved lengthwise

4 eggs

¼ lb (125g) trimmed kale leaves, torn

¾ lb (400g) roasted or grilled chicken, shredded

green goddess dressing

¼ cup (75g) mayonnaise

2 tbsp sour cream

¼ cup coarsely chopped flat-leaf parsley

1 tbsp coarsely chopped basil

1 tbsp coarsely chopped chives

1 tbsp lemon juice

1 garlic clove, finely chopped

salt and freshly ground black pepper

1   To make the green goddess dressing, add ingredients to the bowl of a food processor, combine until smooth. Season with salt and pepper to taste. Set aside.

2   Preheat a cast-iron ridged grill pan to medium heat. Toast the bread on one side, then turn onto the other side and sprinkle with half of the parmesan cheese. Grill until the parmesan cheese melts and is lightly browned. Set aside.

3   Heat the olive oil in a small skillet over medium heat; cook the prosciutto until golden and crisp. Remove from the pan; set aside to drain on paper towels. Cook the asparagus in the same pan, stirring, for 5 minutes or until lightly browned and tender.

4   Place the eggs in a medium saucepan; cover with cold water. Stir gently (this centers the yolks) over high heat until the water comes to a boil. Boil for 4 minutes or until soft-boiled. Drain the eggs; rinse under cold water. Roll the eggs on a work surface, then peel.

5   Meanwhile, put the kale and one-quarter of the green goddess dressing in a large bowl; toss to combine. Allow to stand for 5 minutes to soften the kale slightly.

6   Arrange the kale, toasted bread, chicken, prosciutto, asparagus, remaining parmesan cheese, and halved soft-boiled eggs on a serving dish. Drizzle generously with the remaining green goddess dressing.

TIP

For a meat-free meal, omit the chicken and prosciutto; add some more grilled asparagus or chestnut mushrooms instead.

Smoked salmon salad with Japanese dressing

HEALTHY CHOICE | PREP + COOK TIME **25 MINUTES** | SERVES **6**

A zingy dressing and toasted sesame seeds lift this smoked salmon salad out of the ordinary with very little effort. For a portable lunch, the recipe can be prepared up to 8 hours ahead to the end of step 3; cover and refrigerate the salad ingredients until ready to assemble.

³/₄ lb (340g) asparagus, trimmed, cut into short lengths

2 cups (200g) frozen edamame pods, shelled (see tips)

1 lb (500g) small radishes, thinly sliced (see tips)

1 cucumber (400g), thinly sliced (see tips)

¹/₂ lb (200g) bok choy, separated into leaves

¹/₂ lb (200g) curly endive

2 oz (50g) prepared seaweed salad, optional (see tips)

1 ¹/₄ lbs (600g) smoked salmon slices

2 tsp sesame seeds, toasted

salt and freshly ground black pepper

Japanese dressing

1 tbsp grated fresh ginger

¹/₄ cup (60ml) extra virgin olive oil

¹/₄ cup (60ml) mirin

¹/₄ cup (60ml) soy sauce

2 tbsp lime juice

1 tbsp light brown sugar

1 small red chile, seeded, finely chopped

TIPS

▪ You will need ¹/₂ cup (100g) shelled edamame. Use a V-slicer or mandoline to thinly slice the radishes and cucumber, if you have one.

▪ Seaweed salad is available at your grocery store sushi counter or from your favorite Japanese market.

▪ You can use smoked sea trout instead of the salmon and watercress, or spinach leaves instead of the bok choy and endive, if you like.

1 Cook the asparagus and edamame in a medium saucepan of boiling water for 30 seconds or until just tender. Remove with a slotted spoon. Refresh in a bowl of iced water; drain and set aside.

2 To make the Japanese dressing, press the ginger between 2 spoons over a small bowl to extract the juice; discard the pulp. Transfer the ginger juice to a small screw-top jar with a tight-fitting lid. Add the remaining dressing ingredients; shake well to combine.

3 Put the radish, cucumber, bok choy, endive, asparagus, edamame, and seaweed salad, if using, in a large bowl. Mix to combine.

4 Transfer the salad to a platter or divide evenly among 6 plates; top with the salmon. Drizzle the salad with the Japanese dressing, and sprinkle with the toasted sesame seeds. Season with salt and pepper to taste.

Chickpea tabbouleh with beets

MEAT-FREE | PREP + COOK TIME **20 MINUTES** | SERVES **6**

A Middle Eastern salad especially popular in Lebanon, tabbouleh is usually made with bulgur wheat. Cooked chickpeas are used here instead, cutting down preparation time by avoiding the need for soaking. A simple yogurt dressing adds the characteristic lemony acidity.

2 x 15 oz cans chickpeas (550g), drained, rinsed

$\frac{1}{2}$ lb (225g) cherry vine tomatoes, halved

1 cup (200g) cooked, peeled, julienned beet

$\frac{1}{2}$ cup (150g) thinly sliced red onion

2 tbsp extra virgin olive oil

$\frac{1}{2}$ cup (50g) walnuts, roasted, chopped

$\frac{1}{2}$ cup (15g) firmly packed flat-leaf parsley leaves

$\frac{1}{2}$ cup (15g) firmly packed mint leaves

1 tsp grated lemon zest (see tip)

salt and freshly ground black pepper

lemon-yogurt dressing

$\frac{1}{2}$ cup (140g) Greek-style yogurt

$\frac{1}{2}$ tsp finely grated lemon zest

1 tbsp lemon juice

1 In a food processor, chop the chickpeas using the pulse button until finely chopped to about the size of barley.

2 Meanwhile, to make the lemon-yogurt dressing, combine the ingredients in a small bowl; season with salt and pepper to taste. Set aside.

3 Put the chickpeas, tomatoes, beets, onion, olive oil, walnuts, parsley, and mint in a large bowl; toss gently to combine. Season with salt and pepper to taste. Drizzle with the lemon-yogurt dressing, and sprinkle over the lemon zest.

TIPS

• Use a julienne peeler to shred the beet into fine julienne more easily.

• You could use a zesting tool to create strips of lemon zest instead of grating. If you don't have one, use a vegetable peeler to remove the zest, avoiding the white pith, then cut the zest into long, thin strips.

Mango slaw with chile-lime dressing

HEALTHY CHOICE | PREP + COOK TIME **25 MINUTES + STANDING** | SERVES **8 AS A SIDE**

This fragrant Thai-inspired slaw is at once sour, sweet, and salty, and delightfully crisp.
Add the dressing at the last minute before serving, to keep the salad at its crispest. It can
be eaten as is or added to sliced ham or pork for a delicious sandwich.

³/₄ lb (300g) red cabbage, thinly sliced

1 large carrot (180g), peeled, julienned

2 lbs (800g) green or underripe mango, peeled,
julienned (see tip)

5 shallots, thinly sliced

1 cup (150g) frozen shelled edamame, thawed

¹/₃ cup (10g) firmly packed mint leaves

¹/₃ cup (10g) Thai basil leaves

¹/₄ cup (40g) sesame seeds, toasted

chile-lime dressing

¹/₃ cup (80ml) lime juice

2 tbsp grapeseed oil

1 tbsp fish sauce

2 tbsp (30g) sugar

2 long red chiles, seeded, finely chopped

salt and freshly ground black pepper

1 Spread the cabbage, in a single layer, over a baking sheet. Allow to stand at room temperature for 30 minutes to dry (this will help to stop the color from bleeding into the rest of the salad).

2 Put the cabbage, carrot, mango, shallots, edamame, herbs, and sesame seeds in a large bowl.

3 To make the chile-lime dressing, put the ingredients in a screw-top jar with a tight-fitting lid. Shake well until the sugar dissolves. Season with salt and pepper to taste.

4 Just before serving, drizzle the chile-lime dressing over the salad; toss gently to combine.

TIPS

▪ If you want a creamy slaw, add a little Japanese mayonnaise to the dressing.

▪ To make this salad vegetarian, swap the fish sauce for soy sauce.

▪ You can use either green papaya or jicama instead of the mango if you'd prefer.

Asparagus with crisp lentils and herby yogurt

MEAT-FREE | PREP + COOK TIME **30 MINUTES** | SERVES **6**

The lentils in this recipe are cooked until crisp, taking on a different life both as a protein and as a crunchy topping to add layers of contrasting texture with the tender fresh asparagus and creamy dressing. This technique can also be used with canned butterbeans.

2 x 14 oz (400g) cans brown lentils, drained, rinsed

$^1/_3$ cup (80ml) extra virgin olive oil

1 garlic clove, crushed

1 long red chile, seeded, finely chopped

1 lemon (140g)

1$^1/_4$ lbs (680g) asparagus, trimmed

salt and freshly ground black pepper

herb yogurt

1 cup (280g) Greek-style yogurt

1 cup (25g) firmly packed flat-leaf parsley leaves

$^1/_4$ cup (6g) tarragon

2 tbsp lemon juice

1 Pat the lentils dry with paper towels. Heat the oil in a large sauté pan over medium-high heat. Cook the garlic and chile for 30 seconds until fragrant. Add the lentils; cook, stirring, for 15 minutes or until the lentils are crisp. Season with salt and pepper to taste. Remove the lentils from the pan, and set aside to drain on paper towels.

2 Remove strips of zest from the lemon using a zesting tool; place in a bowl of cold water.

3 Put half of the asparagus in a steamer, bamboo steamer, or round wire rack over a wok or wide pan containing about $^3/_4$ inches of water. Steam the asparagus, covered, for 1 minute; transfer to a plate. Season with salt and pepper to taste. Repeat with the remaining asparagus.

4 Meanwhile, to make the herb yogurt, pulse half of the yogurt, parsley, tarragon, and lemon juice in a small food processor until smooth. Transfer to a small bowl; stir in the remaining yogurt; season with salt and pepper to taste.

5 Spoon some of the herb yogurt onto a platter. Top with the asparagus, then sprinkle with the crisp lentils. Spoon over more of the herb yogurt; top with the lemon zest strips. Serve with the remaining herb yogurt for spooning over.

TIP

The herb yogurt can be made up to a day ahead and refrigerated until needed.

Fast salads

Fresh, fast, and balanced in flavor and whole-food nutrition, these salads make great go-to options when you need to get food on the table fast or are looking for inspiration for a portable lunch. Colorful and appealing, they also work well as part of a larger meal.

Moroccan vegetable salad

PREP TIME **20 MINUTES** | SERVES **4**

Using the shredder attachment on a food processor, grate 2 raw, peeled beets, 1 bunch of radishes, 2 zucchinis, and 1 large carrot; tip the vegetables onto a platter. Wipe the food processor bowl clean. Process $^1/_3$ cup (80ml) extra virgin olive oil, 2 tablespoons pomegranate molasses, 2 tablespoons lemon juice, $^1/_2$ teaspoon each of ground cumin, sumac, and salt to taste until combined. Drizzle half of the dressing over the vegetables. Rinse and drain a 15 oz can (425g) chickpeas; combine with the remaining dressing and 8 oz (250g) halved cherry tomatoes in a medium bowl. Top the salad with the chickpea mixture; sprinkle with $^1/_2$ cup (10g) loosely packed mint leaves. Serve with $1^1/_2$ cups pita chips.

Vietnamese chicken salad

PREP TIME **30 MINUTES** | SERVES **4**

Using the shredder attachment on a food processor, grate $^1/_2$ lb (225g) green cabbage; transfer to a small bowl. Grate 1 large carrot; tip into a large bowl. Add 1 thinly sliced red onion, $^1/_2$ cup (125ml) rice wine vinegar, 2 teaspoons salt, and 2 tablespoons sugar; allow to stand for 5 minutes. Add $1^1/_2$ cups (175g) bean sprouts; allow to stand for 3 minutes. Drain the pickled vegetables; return to the bowl. Add the cabbage, 1 lb (500g) shredded cooked chicken breast, and $^1/_3$ cup each of mint and cilantro leaves. Put $^1/_4$ cup (60ml) water, 1 crushed garlic clove, 2 tablespoons each of fish sauce, sugar, and lime juice in a screw-top jar; shake well. Pour the dressing over the salad; toss to combine. Sprinkle with 2 tablespoons each of crushed salted roasted cashews and fried shallots.

Salad of crunchy things

PREP + COOK TIME **20 MINUTES** | SERVES **4**

In a small skillet over medium heat, stir 1 tablespoon olive oil and 2 tablespoons each of sesame seeds, sunflower seeds, and pepitas for 5 minutes until golden. Add 2 teaspoons chia seeds and 1 tablespoon tamari; stir to combine. Remove from the heat. Using the shredder attachment on a food processor, grat 2 peeled kohlrabi and $^3/_4$ lb (400g) trimmed Brussels sprouts. Tip the vegetables into a large bowl. Process 4 curly kale leaves until coarsely chopped; add to the bowl with $^3/_4$ cup (15g) loosely packed flat-leaf parsley leaves. Process $^1/_4$ cup (60ml) extra virgin olive oil, 2 tablespoons lemon juice, 1 crushed garlic clove, and 2 teaspoons Dijon mustard; season with salt and pepper to taste. Add to the vegetables, and toss through. Top with the crunchy seed mixture.

Red salad

PREP TIME **30 MINUTES** | SERVES **4**

Using the slicer attachment on a food processor, slice 1 red onion and $^1/_2$ red cabbage. Whisk together $^2/_3$ cup (80ml) white wine vinegar and $^1/_4$ cup (55g) sugar in a large bowl until the sugar dissolves. Add the cabbage mixture; allow to stand for 20 minutes. Drain and discard any excess dressing from the bowl; season the vegetable mixture with salt and freshly ground black pepper to taste. Cut $^1/_2$ lb (250g) precooked beets into wedges. Cut 2 small radicchio into thin wedges; arrange on a platter with the beet and cabbage mixture. Crumble over 5 oz (150g) goat cheese; top with $^1/_4$ cup (40g) coarsely chopped dry-roasted almonds and $^1/_4$ cup (15g) chopped chives. Drizzle with 1 tablespoon extra virgin olive oil.

Smoked trout and pickled vegetable buns

HEALTHIER CHOICE | PREP + COOK TIME **20 MINUTES + REFRIGERATION** | SERVES **6**

Quick-pickled vegetables add crunch and a sharp tang to these rolls. To make the recipe an even healthier choice, choose a whole-grain roll and, depending on your dietary preferences, substitute the fish for smoked chicken or even marinated tofu, if you like.

6 sandwich rolls, halved

1 cup (240g) cream cheese, softened

1 head butter lettuce (180g), leaves separated

1 lb (480g) hot-smoked trout or salmon fillets, flaked

pickled veg

1/3 cup (80ml) lemon juice

2 tbsp sugar

2 tbsp finely chopped fresh dill

1 tbsp mustard seeds, toasted

1 tbsp white wine vinegar

2 tsp sea salt flakes

8 small radishes (280g), thinly sliced

1/2 cup (100g) thinly sliced red onion

4 baby cucumbers (160g), thinly sliced lengthwise

freshly ground black pepper

1 To make the pickled veg, put the lemon juice, sugar, dill, mustard seeds, vinegar, and sea salt in a medium glass or nonreactive bowl. Whisk together until the sugar dissolves. Add the radishes, onion, and cucumbers. Season with pepper to taste; toss to combine. Cover the pickles; refrigerate for 30 minutes to allow the flavors to develop. Drain, discarding the pickling liquid.

2 Spread the sandwich roll bases with the cream cheese; layer with the lettuce, trout, and pickled vegetables. Top with the lids.

3 Arrange the buns on a large platter, and serve immediately.

TIPS

- Use a mandoline or V-slicer, available from kitchenware stores, to thinly slice the vegetables.
- For decoration and ease of handling, secure the sandwiches with toothpicks.

Roasted chickpea and carrot salad with feta

MEAT-FREE | PREP + COOK TIME **30 MINUTES** | SERVES **1**

To speed preparation, get the carrots into the oven first. While they are cooking, pick the herbs so they're ready to use. You could make a double quantity, and take the other half to lunch the following day—or bulk up the quantities even more to serve family or friends.

½ lb (200g) baby carrots, trimmed

1 15 oz can (425g) can chickpeas, drained, rinsed

2 tbsp extra virgin olive oil

1 tsp finely grated lemon zest

1½ tsp cumin seeds, lightly crushed

1½ tsp coriander seeds, lightly crushed

1½ tsp fennel seeds, lightly crushed

½ cup (10g) loosely packed mint leaves

½ cup (10g) loosely packed flat-leaf parsley

¼ cup (6g) loosely packed dill sprigs

2 tbsp lemon juice

4 oz (100g) drained marinated feta, plus 1 tbsp of the marinating oil

salt and freshly ground black pepper

crusty bread, to serve

1   Preheat the oven to 425°F. Line a baking sheet with parchment paper.

2   Combine the carrots, chickpeas, oil, lemon zest, and seeds on the baking sheet; season with salt and pepper to taste. Roast in the oven for 25 minutes or until the carrots are golden and tender. Transfer the carrots to a serving bowl.

3   In a small bowl, combine the mint, parsley, and dill. Drizzle with the lemon juice; season with salt and pepper to taste. Sprinkle the herbs over the carrot and chickpea mixture. Top with the feta, then drizzle with a little of the marinating oil. Accompany with crusty bread.

TIP

If you buy a bunch of carrots with the green tops attached, trim them off before you put the carrots in the vegetable crisper of the refrigerator. This helps to extend their shelf life.

Cheesy chorizo quesaditas

KID-FRIENDLY | PREP + COOK TIME **20 MINUTES** | MAKES **2**

Oozing with cheese and spicy, paprika-laden chorizo, these mini quesadillas are simple to put together. Baby spinach, onion, and red pepper provide balance in both flavor and texture. The end result: a hearty lunch in its own edible container.

1 tbsp olive oil

¼ cup (75g) small red onion, finely chopped

½ lb (225g) Spanish chorizo, finely chopped

1 tsp smoked paprika

⅓ cup (80g) chopped drained roasted red pepper in oil

2 whole-grain pita pocket breads

½ cup (50g) grated mozzarella

½ cup (50g) grated Monterey jack cheese

½ cup (20g) spinach leaves

salt and freshly ground black pepper

1   Heat the olive oil in a medium frying pan over medium-high heat; cook the onion, stirring, for 3 minutes or until softened. Add the chorizo; cook for 2 minutes. Add the paprika; cook for 30 seconds. Stir in the red pepper; season with salt and pepper to taste.

2   Warm the pita bread in a microwave for 15 seconds to refresh. Split the pita pockets open. Fill each with a quarter of the cheese, half of the chorizo mixture, and half of the spinach, then top with the remaining cheese.

3   Toast the sandwiches in a hot, dry skillet pressing with a weight or the bottom of another skillet for 4 minutes or until golden and crisp. Serve immediately.

4   Preheat a sandwich press until hot. Toast the quesaditas in the sandwich press for 4 minutes or until golden and crisp. Serve immediately.

TIP

For a portable lunch, wrap the quesaditas in parchment paper and pack in airtight containers. For a more traditional quesadilla, substitute 4 x 8-inch flour tortillas for the pita bread.

Spicy miso dumpling soup

ONE-POT | PREP + COOK TIME **15 MINUTES** | SERVES **2**

Shiro miso is subtler and more delicate than darker miso varieties. Along with chile and ginger, it provides the defining flavor in this delicious, fast-to-whip-up soup. If you would like to up the vegetable quota, try adding broccoli florets or snow peas.

2 tbsp shiro miso (white miso) paste

1 long red chile, thinly sliced

1 tsp finely grated fresh root ginger

2 tsp light soy sauce

10 frozen pork gyoza

$^1/_4$ lb (150g) baby bok choi, quartered

1 green onion, thinly sliced diagonally

1 tsp sesame seeds, toasted

1 Put 3 cups (750ml) water and the shiro miso, chile, ginger, and soy sauce in a small saucepan over medium heat. Bring to a simmer, stirring occasionally, until well combined.

2 Add the gyoza; cook for 6 minutes or until heated through. Add the bok choi; cook for a further 2 minutes. Spoon into 2 serving bowls. Serve topped with the green onion and toasted sesame seeds.

TIPS

- You can use vegetarian or chicken gyoza instead of the pork, if you like.
- Miso paste will keep stored in the fridge for up to 3 months and can be used in marinades, stir-fries, and dressings.

WEEKNIGHT FEASTS

These tempting dishes are high in culinary comfort, but low on fuss—just what's needed at the end of a hectic day, whether you're cooking for one or feeding a hungry horde.

Dukkah shrimp skewers with labneh and minty tomato salad

HEALTHY CHOICE/GLUTEN-FREE | PREP + COOK TIME **30 MINUTES** | SERVES **4**

Dukkah is an Egyptian spice mixture made of roasted nuts, seeds, and an array of spices. Used as a condiment, dip, or seasoning, variations abound—sometimes even from family to family. In this recipe we've used one that features pistachios, but any dukkah will work.

1/4 cup (35g) pistachio dukkah

2 tbsp extra virgin olive oil

2 garlic cloves, crushed

2 tsp finely grated lemon zest

1 1/2 lbs (600g) large, raw shrimp

10 oz (280g) labneh

1 lemon (140g), cut into wedges

salt and freshly ground black pepper

minty tomato salad

3/4 cup (400g) mixed baby heirloom tomatoes, coarsely chopped

1 cup (25g) firmly packed flat-leaf parsley leaves

1/2 cup (15g) firmly packed mint leaves

2 tbsp red wine vinegar

1 tbsp garlic oil

salt and freshly ground black pepper

1 Combine the dukkah, oil, garlic, and lemon zest in a large bowl. Add the shrimp; toss to coat in the dukkah mixture. Add salt and pepper to taste.

2 Preheat a cast-iron ridged grill pan over high heat. Thread the shrimp onto 8 bamboo skewers. Cook the skewers on a heated oiled grill plate for 3–4 minutes until the shrimp change color and are just cooked.

3 Meanwhile, to make the minty tomato salad, put the ingredients in a large bowl; toss gently to combine. Season with salt and pepper to taste.

4 Serve the shrimp skewers with the salad, labneh, and lemon wedges for squeezing over.

TIPS

- You can use fresh shrimp if you like. Simply use 2 1/2 lbs of shrimp, steam in the shells, then peel and devein.
- If you have a nut allergy, substitute the dukkah with 2 teaspoons sumac or chopped flat-leaf parsley.
- Soak skewers in boiling water for 10 minutes before adding the shrimp to prevent scorching.

Bacon and corn fritters with avocado dressing

KID-FRIENDLY | PREP + COOK TIME **30 MINUTES** | SERVES **4**

We have paired these fritters with fennel, which has an aniselike taste and crisp texture when raw, making it a great companion to cut through richer flavors such as the bacon and creamy avocado dressing used in this recipe.

¼ lb (125g) thick cut bacon, coarsely chopped

¼ lb (125g) frozen or fresh corn

1 x 14 oz (411g) diced tomatoes, drained

2 garlic cloves, crushed

2 tbsp chopped chives, plus extra 1 tbsp for serving

2 tsp smoked paprika

2 eggs

⅓ cup (80ml) milk

1 cup (150g) spelt flour

½ tsp baking powder

2 tbsp olive oil

1 large fennel bulb (550g), thinly sliced

salt and freshly ground black pepper

lemon halves, to serve (optional)

avocado dressing

2 avocados (300g)

½ cup (150g) mayonnaise

1 tbsp lemon juice

1 garlic clove, crushed

1 Heat a large, nonstick skillet over high heat; cook the bacon until golden and crisp. Transfer to a large bowl.

2 Add the corn, tomatoes, garlic, chives, smoked paprika, eggs, and milk; stir to combine. Sift together the spelt flour and baking powder. Mix well until combined. Season with salt and pepper to taste. Set aside.

3 Meanwhile, to make the avocado dressing, cut each avocado in half lengthwise and remove the pit. Scrape the avocado flesh out of the shell. In the bowl of a food processor, add the avocado, mayonnaise, lemon juice, and garlic until smooth. Season with salt and pepper to taste.

4 Wipe the skillet dry with a paper towel, then return and add the olive oil over medium heat. Spoon 2 tablespoons of the fritter mixture into the pan; cook for 2 minutes or until bubbles appear on top. Turn the fritters; cook for a further 2 minutes until the other side is lightly browned. Repeat with the remaining batter to make 8 fritters in total. Drain on a paper towel.

5 Combine the fennel and extra 1 tablespoon chopped chives in a small bowl. Season with salt and pepper to taste.

6 Serve the fritters with the fennel salad, avocado mixture, and lemon halves for squeezing over, if you like.

TIP

If preparing the fennel ahead, drop it into a bowl of iced water and refrigerate until needed, to avoid browning. Drain and pat dry just before using.

Spinach and ricotta-stuffed chicken

ONE-POT/KID-FRIENDLY | PREP + COOK TIME **30 MINUTES** | SERVES **4**

The topping used for this dish is a classic combination in Italian cooking. The tangy acidity
of the tomato cuts through the rich creaminess of the cheese, melding the two together
to provide the perfect complement to the chicken.

1¹/₂ lbs (750g) frozen sweet potato fries

1¹/₃ cups (320g) fresh ricotta cheese

¹/₄ cup (20g) finely grated Parmesan cheese

5 cups (150g) spinach leaves

8 x ¹/₄ lb (1 kg) chicken cutlets

¹/₄ cup (60ml) olive oil

1 cup (260g) tomato sauce

4 tbsp tomato paste

1 cup (100g) coarsely grated mozzarella

2 tbsp balsamic dressing

sea salt flakes

1   Preheat the oven to 425°F. Line a large baking sheet with parchment paper. Spray the inside of a 9 x 13 inches baking dish with cooking spray.

2   Place the fries on a baking sheet and season with sea salt flakes. Cook in the oven according to the package directions until crisp.

3   Meanwhile, mix together the ricotta and Parmesan cheese. Layer 2 cups (40g) of the spinach and the cheese mixture evenly among the chicken cutlets, leaving a ¹/₂ in border around the edges. Roll up to enclose the filling; secure with toothpicks.

4   Heat the olive oil in a large skillet over medium heat. Cook the chicken, in batches, for 2 minutes on each side or until golden. Remove with a slotted spoon; drain on paper towels.

5   In a small saucepan, add the tomato sauce and tomato paste over low heat. Stir until combined. Season with salt and pepper to taste.

6   Arrange the chicken in a single layer in the baking dish; top with the tomato sauce mixture and mozzarella. Bake for 10 minutes or until the cheese melts and the chicken is cooked through.

7   Toss the remaining spinach with the balsamic dressing in a large bowl.

8   Serve the chicken with the sweet potato fries and spinach salad.

TIPS

- Remove the toothpicks from the chicken before serving.
- If chicken cutlets are unavailable, cut 4 large skinless boneless chicken breasts in half horizontally, to make 8 cutlets, then pound between plastic wrap until even and ¹/₄ in thick.

Rosemary turkey skewers

HEALTHY CHOICE | PREP + COOK TIME **30 MINUTES** | SERVES **4**

We've used ground turkey meat for the skewers here, proof that this wonderfully healthy meat shouldn't be reserved just for Thanksgiving! The rosemary skewers will infuse flavor into the meat during cooking; alternatively you can use soaked bamboo skewers and add 2 teaspoons finely chopped rosemary to the mixture, if you like.

8 sprigs of rosemary

1¼ lbs (600g) ground turkey

1 egg

2 garlic cloves, crushed

1 tbsp tomato paste

1 cup (70g) stale bread crumbs

2 tbsp extra virgin olive oil

¾ cup (200g) thinly sliced onion

1 tbsp flour

1 cup (250ml) beef stock

2 tomatoes (300g), coarsely chopped

3 cups (475g) microwave or instant white or brown rice

½ lb (225g) green beans, trimmed

1 Remove two-thirds of the leaves from the bottom part of each rosemary sprig to make skewers. Finely chop 2 teaspoons of the leaves; reserve.

2 Combine the turkey, egg, garlic, tomato paste, bread crumbs, and reserved chopped rosemary in a medium bowl. Mold the turkey mixture into sausage shapes around the rosemary skewers.

3 Preheat an oiled ridged cast-iron grill pan to medium-high heat. Cook the skewers, turning, for 10 minutes or until browned and cooked through. Remove from the pan; cover and set aside to keep warm.

4 Meanwhile, heat the olive oil in a large skillet over medium heat; cook the onion, stirring, until soft. Add the flour; cook, stirring, until the mixture bubbles and thickens. Gradually stir in the stock until smooth. Add the tomato paste; cook, stirring, until the gravy thickens.

5 At the same time, heat the rice according to the package directions. Microwave the green beans on HIGH (100%) for 1 minute or until tender.

6 Serve the skewers with the gravy, rice, and green beans.

Soy-glazed salmon with greens

HEALTHY CHOICE | PREP + COOK TIME **25 MINUTES** | SERVES **1**

Cooking fish with the skin on can be helpful in keeping the fish moist during cooking and therefore protecting it from being overdone. The skin can always be removed afterward, if you prefer, as we've done in the recipe here.

1/4 cup (60ml) soy sauce

2 tbsp sugar

2 tsp finely grated fresh ginger root

1 tsp sesame oil

2 tbsp rice wine vinegar

1/2 lb (225g) salmon fillet, skin on

2 stems of broccolini (55g), coarsely chopped

1/2 cup (50g) sugar snap peas

1/4 cup (40g) frozen garden peas, thawed

2 tbsp cilantro, coarsely chopped, plus extra leaves, to serve

2 green onions, thinly sliced diagonally

1 tsp sesame seeds, toasted

steamed brown rice, to serve (optional)

1 Preheat the oven to 425°F. Line a baking sheet with parchment paper.

2 In a small saucepan, combine the soy sauce, sugar, ginger, sesame oil, and half of the vinegar; cook the marinade, over a high heat, for 4 minutes or until thickened.

3 Place the salmon on the baking sheet, skin side up; brush half of the marinade over both sides of the salmon. Roast in the oven for 8 minutes or until golden and almost cooked through.

4 Meanwhile, bring a large saucepan of salted water to a boil. Add the broccolini; cook for 1 minute. Add the sugar snap peas and garden peas; cook for a further minute or until the vegetables are tender crisp. Drain well; transfer to a serving bowl with the cilantro and green onions.

5 Flake the salmon, discarding the skin. Add to a bowl with the remaining marinade and vinegar; toss gently to combine.

6 Top with the sesame seeds and extra cilantro, and serve with steamed brown rice, if you like.

Lamb chops with peach caprese salad

GLUTEN-FREE | PREP + COOK TIME **25 MINUTES** | SERVES **4**

This main-course spin-off of the Italian classic caprese salad includes succulent peaches and a vibrant, minty pesto. With its fresh mix of flavors and textures that bring summer to your plate, it is ideal for informal eating or a long, lazy lunch, yet so easy to prepare.

1³/₄ lbs (800g) lamb loin chops

1¹/₂ tbsp extra virgin olive oil

4 peaches (600g), thickly sliced

¹/₂ lb (225g) buffalo mozzarella, torn

³/₄ lb (400g) vine tomatoes, halved

¹/₂ cup (10g) basil leaves

1 tbsp white wine vinegar

salt and freshly ground black pepper

pistachio-mint pesto

1¹/₂ cups (35g) firmly packed mint leaves

1 cup (25g) firmly packed flat-leaf parsley leaves

¹/₂ cup (75g) pistachios

1 garlic clove, crushed

2 tsp finely grated lemon zest

2 tsp lemon juice

¹/₂ cup (125ml) extra virgin olive oil

1 To make the pistachio-mint pesto. In the bowl of a food processor, combine the ingredients until smooth; season with salt and pepper to taste.

2 Combine the lamb chops and 1 tablespoon of the olive oil in a medium bowl; season with salt and pepper to taste. Preheat a cast iron ridged grill pan over high heat. Cook the lamb for about 3 minutes on each side, adding the peaches to the grill for the last 2 minutes of the lamb cooking time, or until the lamb is cooked as desired and the peaches are golden and grill marks appear.

3 Layer the peaches with the mozzarella, tomatoes, and basil; drizzle with the combined vinegar and remaining oil. Serve the salad with the lamb and pistachio-mint pesto.

TIPS

▪ Buffalo mozzarella has a tangier flavor than cow's milk mozzarella, which may be substituted for it.

▪ For a nut-free pesto, use pepitas (pumpkin seeds) instead of the pistachios.

Lemongrass and lime shrimp with broccoli rice

GLUTEN-FREE | PREP + COOK TIME **15 MINUTES** | SERVES **4**

This low-carb recipe replaces white rice with a plant-based rice made from broccoli to accompany the zesty shrimp. You could also make this using cauliflower rice. The earthy, slightly bitter flavor of both these vegetables complements the sweetness of the shrimp.

1 lb (500g) broccoli, finely chopped

5 tbsp (80g) butter

4 in stalk (20g) fresh lemongrass, finely chopped

1 lb (500g) raw shrimp, peeled and deveined

1 tbsp finely grated lime zest

2 tbsp lime juice

2 tbsp finely chopped cilantro

2 green onions, thinly sliced

salt and freshly ground black pepper

2 limes, halved, to serve

1   In the bowl of a food processor, add the broccoli and process in batches, until finely chopped and resembling rice grains. Blanch in a medium saucepan of boiling water for 20 seconds; drain. Spread out the broccoli on paper towels to dry; season with salt and pepper to taste. Spread out in a 9 x 9 or 6 x 9 inches baking dish. Cover to keep warm.

2   Melt the butter in a large skillet over medium heat; cook the lemongrass, stirring, for 1 minute until fragrant. Increase the heat to high; add the shrimp and half of the lime zest. Cook, stirring, for 2–3 minutes until the shrimp change color. Remove from the heat; stir in the lime juice and cilantro.

3   Top the broccoli rice with the shrimp mixture, remaining lime zest, and green onions. Serve with the lime halves for squeezing over.

Thai chicken omelets

HEALTHY CHOICE | PREP + COOK TIME **30 MINUTES** | SERVES **4**

These lacy omelets are made by drizzling the egg mixture into a wok. You could also put the
egg mixture in a squeeze bottle if you have one, and use a small frying pan in place of a wok.
Delicate enoki mushrooms impart a milder flavor here than other, earthier mushrooms.

2 tbsp peanut oil, divided

¾ lb (400g) boneless, skinless chicken breasts,
thinly sliced

¼ cup (80g) thinly sliced onion

2 garlic cloves, crushed

2 tbsp oyster sauce

8 eggs

1 tsp fish sauce

1 tsp all-purpose soy sauce

4 oz (100g) enoki mushrooms, trimmed

1/2 cup (10g) mint leaves

1/2 cup (15g) Thai basil leaves

1 cup (80g) bean sprouts

2 limes, cut into wedges

1 Heat 2 teaspoons of the peanut oil in a large, heavy skillet or wok over
   high heat; stir-fry the chicken, in batches, for 3 minutes or until browned.
   Remove from the wok and set aside.

2 Heat another 2 teaspoons of the peanut oil; stir-fry the onion and garlic
   for 1 minute until fragrant. Return the chicken to the pan with the oyster
   sauce; stir-fry until hot. Remove from the pan; cover to keep warm while
   making the omelets.

3 Whisk together the eggs, fish sauce, and soy sauce in a large bowl. Heat
   1 teaspoon of the peanut oil in the same pan, still over high heat. Ladle
   the egg mixture in a plastic zip-top bag. Snip a small hole in one corner
   and drizzle 1/4 cup of the egg mixture into the heated pan; cook until
   almost set (this happens nearly instantly). Transfer the omelet to
   a serving plate; cover to keep warm. Repeat the cooking to make a total
   of 8 omelets.

4 Fill the omelets with the chicken mixture, enoki mushrooms, mint, Thai
   basil, and bean sprouts. Serve with the lime wedges for squeezing over.

TIPS

- Enoki mushrooms have clumps of long,
spaghetti-like stems with tiny, snowy white caps.
They are available from Asian food stores and
supermarkets. To trim them, cut off the base clump,
leaving the stems long.
- You can use cilantro if Thai basil is unavailable.
- If you like it spicy, add some sliced red chile
to your chicken omelets before serving.

Bacon and herb lamb patties

KID-FRIENDLY | PREP + COOK TIME **25 MINUTES** | MAKES **8**

Taking this recipe one step further to make a patty roll couldn't be simpler. Spread a fresh bread roll (or a pita pocket or wrap) with extra tomato chutney or even hummus, and add a sliced patty, either warm or cold, with some salad.

1 garlic clove, crushed

2 green onions, finely chopped

1 lb (500g) lean ground lamb

1 egg

$^3/_4$ cup (50g) whole-grain bread crumbs

2 tbsp finely chopped flat-leaf parsley

2 tbsp finely chopped oregano

$^1/_3$ cup (110g) tomato chutney

8 slices (200g) thick-cut bacon

2 tbsp olive oil

salt and freshly ground black pepper

2 cups (60g) watercress, sprigs picked, to serve

1 In a large bowl, combine the garlic, onion, lamb, egg, bread crumbs, herbs, and chutney; season with salt and pepper to taste. Shape the mixture into 8 patties. Wrap each patty in a slice of bacon. Secure with toothpicks.

2 Heat the olive oil in a large skillet over medium heat. Cook the patties for 3 minutes on each side or until browned and cooked through. Remove and discard the toothpicks. Serve the warm patties with the watercress alongside.

TIP

Freeze individual cooked and cooled patties in airtight containers for up to 1 month. Thaw overnight in the fridge; reheat in the microwave at work, or eat at room temperature, if taking to school.

Mongolian beef with noodles

ONE-PAN | PREP + COOK TIME **25 MINUTES** | SERVES **4**

Achieving a great stir-fry involves two key steps. First, ensure you have everything ready before you start cooking, so that once the first ingredient hits the wok, the process is seamless. Secondly, don't crowd the wok with the meat or it will stew rather than brown.

1¼ lbs (600g) beef tenderloin, thinly sliced

⅓ cup (80ml) mirin

2 tbsp dark soy sauce

2 tbsp sweet chili sauce

2 tbsp vegetable oil, divided

¾ cup (200g) thinly sliced onion

2 garlic cloves, crushed

1 red bell pepper (200g), thinly sliced

½ lb (225g) Swiss chard, cut into 6 in lengths

1 tbsp light brown sugar

1 tsp sesame oil

⅓ cup (80ml) chicken stock

¾ lb (400g) thick hokkien noodles (see tip)

1 Combine the beef with half each of the mirin, soy sauce, and sweet chili sauce in a medium bowl.

2 Heat half of the vegetable oil in a wok over high heat; stir-fry the beef, in batches, for 2 minutes or until browned. Remove from the wok.

3 Heat the remaining vegetable oil in the wok; stir-fry the onion and garlic for 3 minutes or until the onion softens. Add the red pepper and Swiss chard; stir-fry until the vegetables are tender.

4 Return the beef to the wok with the remaining ingredients; stir-fry for 2 minutes until heated through. Serve immediately.

TIP

Broccolini, bok choi, or other Asian greens in place of the Swiss chard would work well in this stir-fry.

Greek spinach and feta pie

MEAT-FREE | PREP + COOK TIME **30 MINUTES** | SERVES **1**

The amount of filling will look like quite a lot, but don't be daunted. Keep in mind that the spinach will wilt during cooking, reducing the volume considerably. Double the recipe and you can reheat the pie in a microwave for lunch the next day.

$^1/_2$ cup (120g) fresh firm ricotta cheese

2 oz (50g) feta cheese, crumbled

1 tsp dried oregano

1 green onion, thinly sliced

1 tbsp finely chopped pitted kalamata olives

$1^1/_4$ cup (40g) spinach leaves, thinly sliced

$^1/_4$ cup (10g) coarsely chopped fresh dill

1 egg, lightly beaten

freshly ground black pepper

1 puff pastry sheet (thawed if frozen)

$^1/_4$ cup (70g) Greek-style yogurt

1 small garlic clove, crushed

green salad, to serve

1 Preheat the oven to 425°F. Line a baking sheet with parchment paper.

2 Combine the ricotta cheese, feta cheese, oregano, onion, olives, spinach, and 2 tablespoons of the dill in a small bowl. Add all but 1 teaspoon of the beaten egg, and mix well. Season with black pepper. (Reserve the remaining egg to brush the pastry.)

3 Using a 10 inch plate or bowl as a guide, cut out a circle from the pastry. Spoon the ricotta mixture over one half of the pastry, leaving a $^3/_4$ inch border around the edge. Brush the border with the reserved beaten egg. Fold the pastry over to enclose the filling; press the edge together to seal. Brush the top with the remaining beaten egg.

4 Place the pie on the prepared baking sheet; bake for 20 minutes or until the pastry is browned.

5 Meanwhile, combine the remaining dill, yogurt, and garlic in a small bowl. Serve the pie with the dill yogurt and a green salad.

TIP

The uncooked pie can be prepared several hours ahead. Store, covered, in the fridge, until needed.

Sesame-crusted chicken with "quickled" slaw

KID-FRIENDLY | PREP + COOK TIME **25 MINUTES + STANDING** | SERVES "

Pickling generally involves quite a bit of waiting, but with our quick pickled— quickled—slaw all the waiting is conveniently done while you prepare the rest of the recipe. With minimum fuss, you've made a crunchy slaw to accompany tender chicken goujons with a crisp coating.

$^2/_3$ cup (100g) flour

2 eggs

1 cup (75g) panko bread crumbs

$^1/_4$ cup (40g) white sesame seeds

$^1/_4$ cup (50g) black sesame seeds

2 lbs (900g) chicken tenderloin strips

vegetable oil for frying

salt and freshly ground black pepper

1 lime, halved, to serve

micro herbs, to serve (optional)

"quickled" slaw

1 cucumber (130g)

$^3/_4$ lb (400g) carrots, trimmed

$^3/_4$ lb (400g) red cabbage

$^1/_2$ cup (125ml) white wine vinegar

1 tbsp sugar

$^1/_2$ tsp sea salt flakes

lime mayonnaise

1 cup (300g) Japanese mayonnaise

2 tsp finely grated lime zest

1 tbsp lime juice

1 To make the "quickled" slaw, using a vegetable peeler, mandoline, or V-slicer, cut the cucumber and carrots lengthwise into long, thin ribbons. Finely shred the cabbage. Combine the vegetables with the remaining ingredients in a large glass or ceramic (nonreactive) bowl; allow to stand for 15 minutes. Drain.

2 Meanwhile, to make the lime mayonnaise, combine the ingredients in a small bowl; season with salt and pepper to taste.

3 Put the flour in a shallow bowl; season with salt and pepper to taste. In another shallow bowl, lightly beat the eggs. Put the bread crumbs and white and black sesame seeds in a third shallow bowl; toss to combine. Coat the chicken tenderloin strips in the flour; dip in the beaten egg, allowing any excess to drip off, then coat in the bread crumb mixture.

4 Heat $^1/_2$ inch vegetable oil in a large frying pan over medium heat. Fry the chicken, in batches and turning frequently, for 3$^1/_2$ minutes or until golden and cooked through. Remove from the pan with a slotted spoon; drain on paper towels.

5 Serve the chicken with the slaw, mayonnaise, and lime halves for squeezing over, sprinkled with micro herbs, if you like.

Honey-lemon shrimp stir-fry

ONE-POT | PREP + COOK TIME **25 MINUTES** | SERVES **4**

For such a seemingly uncomplicated way of getting meals to the table fast, stir-fries can offer outsize rewards in terms of flavor and freshness to relish and enjoy. If you would like to serve this stir-fry as part of a banquet, pair it with the Vietnamese chicken salad on page 44.

1 tsp sesame seeds

2 tbsp vegetable oil, divided

1 lg (1 kg) uncooked medium shrimp, shelled, deveined, tails on

1 cup (300g), onion wedges

1 lb (500g) Napa cabbage, coarsely chopped

1 large carrot (180g), julienned

$\frac{1}{3}$ cup (80ml) lemon juice

2 tbsp honey

20g piece of fresh ginger root, julienned

3 cups (450g) microwave or instant jasmine rice

4 green onions, thinly sliced

$\frac{1}{4}$ cup (10g) firmly packed cilantro

salt and freshly ground black pepper

1 Toast the sesame seeds in a heated wok until lightly browned; remove from the wok. Set aside.

2 Heat 1 tbsp of the vegetable oil in the wok over high heat; stir-fry the shrimp for 2 minutes or until the shrimp change color. Remove from the wok and set aside.

3 Heat the remaining oil in the wok over medium-high heat; stir-fry the onion for 3 minutes or until tender. Return the shrimp to the wok with the Napa cabbage, carrot, lemon juice, honey, and ginger; stir-fry until hot. Season with salt and pepper to taste.

4 Meanwhile, heat the jasmine rice according to the package directions.

5 Serve the stir-fry with the rice, sprinkled with the toasted sesame seeds, green onions, and cilantro.

TIPS

▪ You can make this recipe using whole shrimp if you like. Simply peel and devein them after cooking. You'll need about 2 lbs of whole shrimp.

▪ Use brown rice instead of jasmine, if you like.

▪ If you prefer to cook your own rice instead of using precooked, you will need to do this before starting the stir-fry; allow for extra cooking time.

▪ If using rice you have already cooked and cooled, always make sure it is piping hot after reheating.

Butternut squash samosa fritters

MEAT-FREE | PREP + COOK TIME **30 MINUTES** | SERVES **2**

Use ready-chopped butternut squash, available from supermarkets and some greengrocers, to save time. You could also microwave the squash. The mixture is quite soft so, if time permits, place the patties in the freezer for 10 minutes, to firm before cooking.

½ lb (225g) butternut squash, coarsely chopped

1 cup (125g) microwave or instant brown rice

¼ cup (30g) frozen peas

¼ cup (70g) grated carrot

2 tsp curry powder

1 tsp finely grated fresh ginger root

⅓ cup (25g) bread crumbs

2 tbsp vegetable oil

salt and freshly ground black pepper

to serve

⅓ cup (95g) Greek-style yogurt

2 tbsp hot lime pickle (see tip)

2 tbsp fresh mint leaves

1 Cook the pumpkin in a medium saucepan of boiling water until tender; drain. Return to the pan, and mash until smooth. Stir the unheated rice, peas, carrot, curry powder, ginger, and bread crumbs into the mashed pumpkin. Season with salt and pepper to taste.

2 Using oiled hands, form the mixture into 6 patties of about ¼ cup each. Heat the vegetable oil in a large skillet over medium heat. Cook the patties, in batches, for 2 minutes on each side or until golden. Serve with the yogurt, pickle, and mint leaves. Accompany with a spinach and tomato salad, if you like.

TIP

A condiment made with limes and a characteristic blend of aromatic spices, lime pickle is an Indian specialty that adds a hot and spicy tang to meals.

Fast pasta

Dried pasta, in its many shapes and sizes, is an ideal pantry standby. Ready-made fresh filled pasta is also great for making a speedy, nutritious meal with the addition of just a few ingredients. Remember to keep them on hand in your pantry or on your shopping list.

Mediterranean mac and cheese

PREP TIME + COOK TIME 35 MINUTES | SERVES 4

Cook 12 oz (375g) elbow macaroni in a large saucepan of boiling salted water; drain. Melt 4 tablespoons (60g) butter in a large saucepan over medium heat. Add $1/3$ cup (50g) all-purpose flour; cook, stirring, for 2 minutes or until the mixture thickens. Gradually stir in 3 cups (750ml) milk. Add $1/3$ cup (80ml) tomato paste; stir until the sauce thickens. Preheat the grill to high. Stir the pasta, a drained 10 oz (280g) jar antipasto vegetables, and $1/3$ cup (20g) finely chopped chives into the sauce. Put in a deep 8-cup (2-liter) ovenproof dish. Sprinkle with 1 cup (125g) grated mozzarella, $1/2$ cup (50g) grated cheddar cheese, and 2–3 tablespoons grated Parmesan cheese. Grill until the cheese is melted and golden.

Butternut squash, spinach, and ricotta agnolotti

PREP TIME 25 MINUTES | SERVES 4

Cook $1 1/4$ lb (625g) premade fresh ricotta and spinach agnolotti in a large saucepan of boiling salted water until cooked through; drain. Melt 3 tbsp (50g) butter in same, cleaned pan over medium heat; cook 1 bunch of finely shredded spinach with 1 teaspoon ground cinnamon until wilted. Remove from the pan. Add 4 cups (1kg) prepared butternut squash soup to the pan. Bring to a boil; simmer for 2 minutes. Add $1/2$ cup (125ml) heavy cream, spinach, and agnolotti; stir until combined and heated through. Remove from heat. Allow to stand for 5 minutes. Season with salt and pepper. Serve topped with 2 oz (100g) fresh ricotta cheese and fresh flat-leaf parsley leaves.

Chicken pesto pasta with tomatoes

PREP TIME + COOK TIME 25 MINUTES | SERVES 4

Preheat the broiler to high. Place $1/2$ lg (250g) cherry vine tomatoes with stems on a baking sheet. Drizzle with 1 teaspoon balsamic vinegar; grill for 10 minutes or until the tomato skins begin to split. Meanwhile, cook 12 oz (375g) penne pasta in a large saucepan of boiling salted water until tender; drain, reserving $1/3$ cup (80ml) of the cooking liquid. Return the pasta to the pan with $1/3$ cup (80ml) basil pesto, 2 cups (350g) shredded roast chicken, tomatoes, and reserved cooking liquid. Stir over low heat until heated through. Serve with 2 tablespoons finely grated Parmesan cheese and some basil.

Turkey ragù

PREP TIME 30 MINUTES | SERVES 4

Cook 12 oz (375g) fettuccine in a saucepan of boiling salted water; drain. Heat 1 tablespoon olive oil in a large skillet over high heat; cook 1 finely chopped onion and 2 crushed garlic cloves, stirring, for 3 minutes until soft. Add 1 finely chopped carrot and celery stalk; cook, stirring, for 5 minutes or until just tender. Add 1 lb (500g) ground turkey; cook, stirring, until the turkey changes color. Add $1 3/4$ cups (435ml) tomato sauce, $1/4$ cup (65ml) tomato paste, and $1/2$ cup (125ml) chicken stock; bring to a boil. Reduce the heat; simmer for 15 minutes or until the mixture thickens. Add $1/2$ cup (75g) frozen peas; heat through. Season with salt and pepper. Serve topped with the ragù and $1/3$ cup (25g) shaved Parmesan cheese.

Chana dal with chutney yogurt

MEAT-FREE | PREP + COOK TIME **30 MINUTES** | SERVES **4**

Chana dal is an Indian favorite featuring chickpeas. For this version, whole chickpeas give the dish a chunkier, stewlike texture than regular dal. Batch-cook by doubling the recipe, so you can take the following night off from cooking or take the leftovers to work for lunch.

1 tbsp peanut oil

³/₄ cup (200g) thinly sliced onions

1¹/₂ tsp finely grated fresh ginger root

2 tsp light brown sugar

¹/₃ cup (75g) korma paste

1 tsp ground cumin

1 tsp ground turmeric

1 tsp sweet paprika

1 x 14.5 oz can (411g) can diced tomatoes

8 oz (225g) cherry tomatoes

1 cup (250ml) coconut milk

1 x 14 oz can (397g) brown lentils, drained, rinsed

1 x 15 oz (425g) can chickpeas, drained, rinsed

a few sprigs of cilantro, to serve

roti bread, warmed, to serve

chutney yogurt

²/₃ cup (190g) Greek-style yogurt

1 tbsp mango chutney

1   Heat the peanut oil in a large saucepan over medium heat. Add the onion, ginger, and brown sugar; cook, stirring, for 5 minutes or until soft. Next, add the korma paste and spices; cook, stirring, for 1 minute or until fragrant.

2   Add the canned tomatoes, cherry tomatoes, 1 cup (250ml) water, coconut milk, lentils, and chickpeas to the pan; bring to a boil. Reduce the heat, and simmer for 10 minutes or until the mixture has thickened slightly.

3   Meanwhile, to make the chutney yogurt, swirl together the yogurt and mango chutney in a small bowl.

4   Serve the dal sprinkled with cilantro, dollops of chutney yogurt, and warm roti bread.

TIP

Freeze individual portions of dal in airtight containers for up to 1 month. Thaw the dal overnight in the fridge. If taking it to work, reheat the thawed dal in the microwave just before eating.

Chile and chicken tostada

CHEAT EAT | PREP + COOK TIME **25 MINUTES** | SERVES **2**

A specialty of Mexico and elsewhere in Latin America, tostadas vary in fillings, but all feature a toasted or fried tortilla. This recipe can easily be doubled. For a vegetarian version, replace the chicken in step 3 with a 15 oz (425g) can of rinsed, drained kidney beans.

2 x 12-in flour tortillas or wraps

2 tbsp vegetable oil, plus extra for brushing

2¹/₂ tbsp finely chopped chipotle chile in adobo sauce, divided

1³/₄ (800g) boneless chicken thighs, trimmed

2 ears of corn (400g)

4 large cherry tomatoes (50g), seeded, finely diced

1 lime, quartered

2 tbsp finely chopped cilantro, plus extra ¹/₃ cup (10g)

3 cups (250g) microwave or instant brown rice

¹/₂ cup (40g) thinly sliced red cabbage

1 tbsp sour cream

salt and freshly ground black pepper

1 Preheat the oven to 350°F.

2 To make the tortilla bowls, cut a wedge (3 inches at its top) from each of the tortillas. Brush the tortillas and wedges on both sides with the extra vegetable oil. Place each tortilla in an ovenproof bowl, slightly overlapping the cut edges of the tortillas to form the shape of a bowl. Bake in the oven for 6 minutes. Carefully transfer the tortillas, domed side up, to a small baking sheet with the tortilla wedges; bake for a further 6 minutes or until golden. The tortilla bowls (tostadas) and tortilla wedges will crisp as they cool.

3 Meanwhile, combine 1¹/₂ tablespoons of the chipotle chile and the 2 tablespoons vegetable oil in a small bowl; season with salt to taste. Add the chicken; turn to coat in the mixture.

4 Heat a large skillet over high heat. Add the olive oil and cook the chicken for 4 minutes on each side or until cooked through, adding the corn to the pan during the last 4 minutes of cooking time. Rest the chicken for 5 minutes, then thinly slice the chicken and the corn kernels from the cob.

5 Meanwhile, to make the salsa, combine the remaining chipotle chile, tomatoes, juice of 2 of the lime wedges, and the chopped cilantro in a bowl. Season with salt and pepper to taste.

6 Heat the rice according to the package instructions. Divide the rice among the tostadas; top with the chicken, corn kernels, extra cilantro sprigs, red cabbage, and salsa. Serve with the sour cream and the remaining lime wedges for squeezing over.

TIPS

- Chipotle in adobo is a hot, smoky-flavored Mexican sauce made from chipotles (smoke-dried jalapeño chiles). It is available from supermarkets.
- Store any leftover chipotle in a small screw-top jar in the fridge for up to 1 month.
- To make a chicken burrito, warm the tortillas and wrap around the filling ingredients.

Crisp fish with buckwheat salad

GLUTEN-FREE/HEALTHY CHOICE | PREP + COOK TIME **30 MINUTES** | SERVES **4**

Despite its name, buckwheat is unrelated to wheat and is in fact a seed, making it an ideal choice for gluten-free diets. Buckwheat is processed into groats that are cooked in a similar way as rice; it is also ground as a flour.

2 tbsp peanut oil

¹/₄ cup (45g) rice flour

4 x ¹/₂ lb (800g) firm white fish fillets, skin on

salt and freshly ground black pepper

buckwheat salad

100g snow peas, trimmed

1 tbsp peanut oil

1 tbsp light soy sauce

1 tsp finely grated fresh ginger root

2 tbsp lime juice

2 tsp light brown sugar

1 carrot (120g), julienned

1 cup (80g) bean sprouts

¹/₃ cup (65g) roasted buckwheat groats (see tip)

1 cup (30g) cilantro leaves

1 To make the buckwheat salad, boil, steam, or microwave the snow peas until tender; drain. Rinse under cold water; drain. In a large bowl, combine the peanut oil, soy sauce, ginger, lime juice, and brown sugar in a large bowl; whisk well. Add the snow peas and the remaining ingredients; toss gently. Season with salt and pepper to taste.

2 Heat the oil in a large skillet over medium heat. Put the rice flour in a shallow bowl; season with salt and pepper to taste. Coat the fish in flour; shake off any excess. Cook the fish, skin-side down, for 5 minutes or until golden and crisp; turn and cook for a further 5 minutes or until just cooked through.

3 Serve the fish with the buckwheat salad.

TIP

If you can't find roasted buckwheat groats, roast the kernels in the oven at 350°F for about 5 minutes; cool before using.

Minestrone with beef ravioli

CHEAP EAT/KID-FRIENDLY | PREP + COOK TIME **25 MINUTES** | SERVES **2**

Fresh ravioli is available from the refrigerated section of most supermarkets. For a vegetarian minestrone, use spinach and ricotta ravioli instead. And if you don't have chili oil, sprinkle the soup with a pinch of dried chile flakes for a touch of heat.

2 tsp extra virgin olive oil

4 green onions, finely chopped

1 garlic clove, crushed

2 tsp finely chopped rosemary leaves

1/4 cup (70g) finely chopped carrot

1 celery stalk (50g), finely chopped

1 x 14.5 oz (411g) can diced tomatoes

2 cups (500ml) vegetable stock

1 tsp sugar

5 oz (150g) fresh beef ravioli

2 tbsp shaved Parmesan cheese

1 tsp chili oil

1 tbsp flat-leaf parsley leaves

salt and freshly ground black pepper

crusty bread, to serve

1 Heat the oil in a medium saucepan over medium heat. Cook the onion, garlic, rosemary, carrot, and celery for 5 minutes or until softened.

2 Add the tomatoes, stock, and sugar; season with salt and pepper to taste. Bring to a boil; cook for 5 minutes. Add the ravioli, cook for 5 minutes or until the ravioli is tender.

3 Divide the soup and ravioli evenly between 2 serving bowls. Top with the Parmesan cheese, drizzle with the chili oil, and scatter over the parsley. Serve accompanied by the crusty bread.

TIP

If freezing the soup to use later, don't add the ravioli. Make the soup, then cool and store in a freezer-proof container. Thaw and reheat when needed, then add the ravioli as at step 2, and continue with the recipe.

Rigatoni with arrabbiata and chorizo sauce

KID-FRIENDLY | PREP + COOK TIME **25 MINUTES** | SERVES **4**

"Arrabbiata" means angry in Italian, and here this tomato sauce with a chili kick is combined with spicy chorizo to make a tasty weeknight standard. There's no need to add oil to the frying pan when cooking the chorizo, as sufficient fat will be released during cooking.

1 lb (500g) dried penne or rigatoni pasta

³/₄ lb (300g) cured chorizo, thinly sliced

2 tbsp extra virgin olive oil

³/₄ cup (200g) finely chopped onion

1 tsp dried chili flakes

3 garlic cloves, crushed

1 x 14.5 oz (411g) can crushed tomato

4 tbsp tomato paste

¹/₂ tsp light brown sugar

¹/₂ cup (15g) coarsely chopped flat-leaf parsley

²/₃ cup (50g) finely grated Parmesan cheese

salt

1 Cook the pasta in a large saucepan of salted boiling water until almost tender—about 8 minutes; drain. Return to the pan and set aside.

2 Meanwhile, cook the chorizo in a large frying pan over medium-high heat, turning occasionally, for 2 minutes or until the chorizo is browned. Remove from the pan; set aside to drain on paper towels.

3 Add the olive oil to the same frying pan; cook the onion, chili flakes, and garlic, stirring, for 3 minutes or until the onion softens. Add the crushed tomato, tomato paste, sugar, and 1 cup (250ml) water. Bring to a boil. Reduce the heat to low; simmer, stirring occasionally, for 7 minutes or until the sauce has thickened slightly. Add the chorizo; stir to combine. Cook for 2 minutes or until heated through. Season with salt to taste.

4 Add the arrabbiata sauce and the parsley to the cooked pasta in the pan; stir over medium heat until heated through. Stir in the Parmesan cheese.

Five-spice pork with almonds

HEALTHY CHOICE | PREP + COOK TIME **30 MINUTES** | SERVES **4**

Five-spice powder is based on the Chinese philosophy of balancing the five main flavors of sweet, sour, salt, bitter, and pungent, which correspond with the five elements of earth, wood, water, fire, and metal. The mix contains star anise, fennel seeds, Sichuan pepper, cloves, and cinnamon.

1½ lb (750g) boneless pork chops, thinly sliced

1 tsp garam masala

2 tsp Chinese five-spice powder

2 tbsp peanut oil, divided

1 carrot (120g), julienned

2 garlic cloves, crushed

1 tbsp finely grated fresh root ginger

1¼ lb (600g) baby bok choi, halved lengthwise

1 tbsp sweet chili sauce

¼ cup (60ml) oyster sauce

2 tbsp lime juice

2 tbsp hot water

100g snow peas, trimmed

1 cup (80g) bean sprouts

⅓ cup (55g) blanched almonds, roasted, coarsely chopped

1 lime (65g), cut into wedges

rice noodles or steamed rice, to serve

1 Combine the pork and spices in a large bowl; mix well.

2 Heat 1 tablespoon of the peanut oil in a wok over high heat; stir-fry the pork mixture, in batches, for 2–3 minutes until the pork is browned and tender. Remove from the wok and set aside.

3 Heat the remaining peanut oil in the wok; add the carrot, garlic, and ginger. Stir-fry for 2 minutes, then add the bok choi, sweet chili sauce, oyster sauce, lime juice, and 2 tablespoons hot water; stir-fry for 4 minutes or until the bok choi is tender.

4 Return the pork to the wok with the snow peas; stir-fry until heated through. Serve topped with the bean sprouts and almonds, and with the lime wedges for squeezing over. Accompany with rice noodles or steamed rice.

TIPS

- You can substitute the pork with chicken, lamb, or beef.
- For a nut-free version, use vegetable oil instead of peanut oil, and replace the almonds with Asian fried shallots.

Spiced steaks with grilled eggplant salad

HEALTHY CHOICE | PREP + COOK TIME **15 MINUTES** | SERVES **2**

Pomegranate molasses, made by boiling down pomegranate juice into a thick syrup, has long been used as a seasoning in Persian and other Middle Eastern cuisines. Here, it provides a pleasant sweet–tart tang for the dressing used for the eggplant salad.

2 tbsp extra virgin olive oil, divided

1 tsp ground allspice

1/2 lb eggplant (200g), cut in strips

2 x 1/2 lb (400g) beef ribeye steaks

6 oz fresh tomatoes (180g), roughly chopped

2 green onions, thinly sliced

1/4 cup (5g) mint leaves

2 tsp pomegranate molasses

salt and freshly ground black pepper

1 Heat a ridged cast-iron grill pan over medium-high heat. Put 1 tablespoon of the olive oil and the allspice in a medium bowl. Season with salt and pepper to taste. Toss the eggplant in the mixture to coat; shake off any excess. Next, toss the steaks in the mixture to coat.

2 Cook the steaks for 2 minutes on each side for medium-rare or until cooked to your liking. Remove, cover loosely with foil, and allow to rest for 5 minutes. Add the eggplant to the same pan; cook for 2 minutes on each side or until softened.

3 Meanwhile, divide the tomato, green onion, and mint between 2 serving plates. Whisk together the remaining olive oil and the pomegranate molasses in a small bowl until combined; season with salt and pepper to taste.

4 Slice the steaks and eggplant, and transfer to the serving plates. Drizzle with the pomegranate dressing to serve.

TIPS

- Accompany with whole-grain couscous or flatbread, if you like.
- You can use lamb sirloin chops in place of the beef.

SOMETHING
SPECIAL

For fast inspiration for that indefinable
element to turn a meal into an occasion,
from celebratory meals to dinner parties and
informal entertaining, here are your answers.

Beet tartare with whipped feta

MEAT-FREE | PREP + COOK TIME **20 MINUTES + REFRIGERATION** | SERVES **8**

This is the perfect easy starter to whip up for entertaining, as it can also be made ahead to the end of step 3 and refrigerated a day ahead. It looks and tastes impressive, too, with its ruby-red beets and a balance of sweet, salty, sour, and nutty crunch to tempt the palate.

$\frac{1}{2}$ lb (225g) feta cheese

$\frac{1}{3}$ cup (80g) sour cream

$\frac{1}{4}$ cup (60ml) extra virgin olive oil, divided

2 lbs (1 kg) cooked beets

$\frac{1}{2}$ cup (90g) drained cornichons

1 tbsp horseradish cream sauce

3 tsp vegetarian Worcestershire sauce

2 tsp Dijon mustard

1 tbsp capers in vinegar, chopped

1 tsp caper pickling liquid

2 tbsp pumpkin seeds

salt and freshly ground black pepper

microgreens, to serve

crispbreads or sliced baguette, to serve

1   To make the whipped feta, in the bowl of a food processor, add the feta, sour cream, and 1 tablespoon of the olive oil for 3 minutes or until smooth. Stop the processor and scrape down the side of the bowl with a spatula twice during processing. Transfer to a serving bowl; season with salt and pepper to taste. Cover and refrigerate for 15 minutes to thicken.

2   Cut the beets into $\frac{1}{4}$ inch dice. Finely chop half of the cornichons. Transfer the beets and chopped cornichons to a medium bowl; stir in the remaining olive oil, horseradish cream sauce, Worcestershire sauce, Dijon mustard, capers, and caper pickling liquid. Season with salt and pepper to taste.

3   Spoon the beet mixture onto a large plate or bowl; sprinkle with the pumpkin seeds and microgreens. Serve the tartare with the whipped feta cheese, remaining cornichons, and crispbreads.

TIP

Spread the whipped feta onto the crispbread first, then top with the beet tartare to prevent the beet tartare from falling off the bread.

Jerk salmon with yogurt potatoes

HEALTHY CHOICE | PREP + COOK TIME **20 MINUTES** | SERVES **2**

"Jerk" is the name of the Jamaican dry or wet spice rub used to season fish and chicken; it is also the name of the cooking method, where traditionally the meat is slow-cooked over a fire. Chili and allspice are the two defining spices in the rub, and both feature here.

³/₄ lb (320g) new potatoes, thickly sliced

¹/₃ cup (10g) firmly packed flat-leaf parsley

¹/₃ cup (15g) firmly packed cilantro

1 tsp freshly ground black pepper

1 tsp dried chili flakes

1 tsp ground allspice

2 garlic cloves, crushed

2 tsp finely grated fresh ginger root

¹/₄ cup (60ml) lime juice

¹/₄ cup (60ml) extra virgin olive oil

2 x ¹/₂ lb (400g) skinless salmon fillets

¹/₄ cup (70g) Greek-style yogurt

2 shallots (50g), finely chopped

salt

1 Boil, steam, or microwave the potato until tender; cover to keep warm.

2 Reserve 1 tablespoon each of the parsley and cilantro. In the bowl of a food processor, combine the remaining herbs with the black pepper, chilli flakes, allspice, garlic, ginger, lime juice, and olive oil; process until it forms a paste. Season with salt and pepper.

3 Pour half of the herb mixture over the salmon in a medium bowl; allow to stand for 5 minutes.

4 Heat a medium nonstick skillet over medium heat. Add the undrained salmon; cook, for 2 minutes on each side or until just cooked through (be careful not to overcook).

5 Combine the potato with the yogurt, shallot, and remaining herb mixture. Serve topped with the salmon, and sprinkled with the reserved parsley and cilantro.

TIPS

- You will need 1 lime for this recipe. To help with juicing, roll the lime firmly on a hard surface first.
- You can substitute the ground allspice with ¹/₂ teaspoon ground cinnamon and ¹/₄ teaspoon each of ground cloves and nutmeg.

Grilled steak with anchovy vinaigrette

HEALTHY CHOICE | PREP + COOK TIME **30 MINUTES + STANDING** | SERVES **6**

This flavorful steak is marinated first, before being cooked at a high temperature and doused in a bold vinaigrette to improve its flavor even further. Accompany with a serving of arugula, baby spinach, or watercress.

2³/₄ lb (1.2 kg) skirt steak

2 tbsp extra virgin olive oil

2 tsp garlic powder

2 tsp light brown sugar

1¹/₂ tsp sea salt flakes

1 tsp freshly ground black pepper

¹/₂ lb (250g) cherry tomatoes

anchovy vinaigrette

¹/₃ cup (80ml) extra virgin olive oil

1 shallot, finely chopped

8 anchovy fillets (20g), finely chopped

2 long red chiles, seeded, finely chopped

1 tbsp thyme leaves, finely chopped

2 tsp each of chopped fresh rosemary and oregano

3 garlic cloves, peeled

2 tsp finely grated lemon zest

2 tbsp lemon juice

1 tbsp red wine vinegar

salt and freshly ground black pepper

1 To make the anchovy vinaigrette, heat the olive oil in a small saucepan over medium heat. Cook the shallot for 3 minutes or until softened. Add the anchovies and chiles; cook for 1 minute or until the anchovy is soft. Transfer to a heatproof bowl; stir in the herbs. Grate the garlic into the hot anchovy mixture using a fine grater or microplane rasp grater. Allow to cool. Stir in the lemon zest, lemon juice, and red wine vinegar. Season with salt and pepper to taste.

2 Meanwhile, pat the steak dry with a paper towel. Combine the oil, garlic powder, brown sugar, sea salt, and black pepper in a large stainless-steel or glass bowl. Add the steak to the bowl; rub the oil mixture all over the steak until evenly coated. Allow to stand at room temperature for 20 minutes.

3 Preheat a ridged cast-iron grill pan to high heat. Cook the steak for 4 minutes on each side for medium, or until grill marks appear and the steak is cooked to your liking (see tip). Transfer to a tray, cover loosely with foil, and allow to rest for at least 10 minutes. Barbecue the whole tomatoes for 2 minutes or until softened slightly. Season with salt and pepper to taste.

4 Slice the steak; drizzle with the anchovy vinaigrette. Serve with the barbecued tomatoes.

TIPS

• Skirt is a less expensive steak cut with great flavor, though a little chewy. It benefits from either long, slow cooking or quick searing. Bring to room temperature first, then rest well before serving.

• You can also use rump, sirloin, ribeye, or eye fillet. Cook for 4 minutes on each side for a ³/₄-in thick steak, and about 10 minutes each side for a 2 in one.

Whipped edamame with crisp rice paper crackers

MEAT-FREE | PREP + COOK TIME **30 MINUTES** | SERVES **8**

This dip is a good choice for entertaining. The whipped edamame can be made up to 4 hours ahead and refrigerated. The rice paper crackers can be fried up to 2 hours ahead; store between sheets of paper towel in an airtight container until needed.

4 cups (800g) fresh or frozen shelled edamame (see tips)

1/3 cup (80ml) peanut oil, plus extra for frying

2 tbsp sesame oil

1/3 cup (80ml) mirin

1/3 cup (80ml) rice wine vinegar

1/4 cup (75g) dashi miso paste (see tips)

2 tbsp lemon juice

1 tbsp Japanese mayonnaise

8 in round rice paper wrappers (80g)

1 tsp black sesame seeds (see tips)

micro greens, to serve

1/3 cup (95g) pink pickled ginger, drained

1 Cook the edamame in a large saucepan of boiling water for 5 minutes or until tender; drain. Refresh in a bowl of iced water; drain.

2 In a food processor, pulse the edamame with the edamame with the 1/3 cup (80ml) peanut oil, sesame oil, mirin, rice wine vinegar, dashi miso paste, lemon juice, mayonnaise, and 1/3 cup (80ml) water for 3 minutes or until pale and smooth; stop the processor and scrape the side occasionally. Transfer to a bowl; cover and set aside until needed.

3 Meanwhile, fill a large saucepan one-third full with the extra peanut oil; heat to 350°F (or until a cube of bread dropped into the oil turns golden in 15 seconds). Deep-fry 1 rice paper round at a time for 5 seconds or until puffed. Drain on paper towels.

4 Sprinkle the whipped edamame with the sesame seeds and micro greens. Serve with the pickled ginger and rice paper crackers.

TIPS

- Fresh or frozen shelled edamame are easy to find at your grocery store.
- Look for dashi miso paste, used as the base for miso soup, in the international section of your grocery store.
- Black sesame seeds are available from Asian and Middle Eastern food stores. If unavailable, top with well-toasted white sesame seeds.

Pistachio pilaf with grilled lamb

GLUTEN-FREE | PREP + COOK TIME **30 MINUTES** | SERVES **6**

Lamb cutlets are sweet and succulent, cut as they are from ribs of lamb, and so really don't need much more than a simple seasoning of salt and pepper, paired with quick grilling over not too high a heat, to be at their most tender and juicy.

2 tbsp (30g) butter, chopped

1/2 cup (150g) finely chopped onion

1 tbsp finely chopped fresh ginger root

1 cinnamon stick

4 green cardamom pods, cracked

1/2 tsp ground turmeric

1/4 cup (6g) loosely packed curry leaves

2 cups (400g) uncooked basmati rice

3 cups (750ml) gluten-free chicken stock or water

1 1/4 lb (600g) French-trimmed lamb chops (about 12)

2 tbsp extra virgin olive oil

2 cups (20g) flat-leaf parsley, coarsely torn

2 cups (20g) mint, coarsely torn

1/3 cup (45g) pistachios, coarsely chopped

1/3 cup (55g) dry-roasted almonds, coarsely chopped

2 tbsp dried currants

2 tbsp lemon juice

salt and freshly ground black pepper

lemon wedges, to serve

Greek yogurt, to serve

1 Heat the butter in a large saucepan over medium-high heat. Add the onion; cook, stirring, for 5 minutes or until softened. Next, add the ginger, spices, curry leaves, and basmati rice; stir to combine. Pour in the chicken stock; bring to a boil. Reduce to the lowest heat; cook, covered, for 10 minutes or until most of the liquid is absorbed. Allow to stand, covered, for 5 minutes.

2 Meanwhile, preheat a grill plate (or ridged cast-iron grill pan or barbecue) to medium-high heat. Drizzle the lamb with the olive oil; season with salt and pepper to taste. Cook the lamb for 3 1/2 minutes on each side for medium, or until cooked to your liking.

3 Stir the parsley, mint, pistachios, almonds, currants, and lemon juice into the rice pilaf; season with salt and pepper to taste. Serve the pilaf with the lamb, lemon wedges for squeezing over, and yogurt.

TIPS

- "French-trimmed" refers to the process of cleaning the bone ends of the cutlets of fat and sinew for a clean presentation.
- To tear herbs coarsely, simply use your hands to tear them straight from the bunch. Alternatively, run a knife over the whole bunch, coarsely chopping both leaves and stems at the same time.

Snapper in banana leaves with Thai herb salad

HEALTHY CHOICE | PREP + COOK TIME **30 MINUTES + STANDING** | SERVES **4**

Wrapping fish in banana leaves helps to keep it moist and holds in the flavors of the other ingredients so that they permeate the whole fish. This technique for marinating fish and meat is found across Southeast Asia, as well as in other tropical regions of the world.

2 tbsp Thai red curry paste

4 garlic cloves, crushed

2 makrut lime leaves, finely chopped

$^1/_3$ cup (80ml) lime juice

2 tbsp fish sauce

$^1/_2$ cup (135g) light brown sugar

$3^1/_4$ lb (1.5kg) whole snapper or mackerel, cleaned

8 banana leaves

Thai herb salad

8 oz (225g) cherry tomatoes, halved

2 green onions, thinly sliced

1 cup (30g) cilantro

$^1/_2$ cup (15g) Thai basil leaves

$^1/_2$ cup (10g) mint leaves

2 tbsp lime juice

2 tbsp fish sauce

1 tbsp peanut oil

$^1/_3$ cup (90g) light brown sugar

1 Heat the red curry paste in a small saucepan at medium heat for 2 minutes or until fragrant. Remove from the heat; stir in the garlic, lime leaves, lime juice, fish sauce, and brown sugar until combined.

2 Rinse the fish; pat dry with paper towels. Cut diagonal slashes in the fish $^3/_4$ inch apart on both sides.

3 Spoon half of the curry paste mixture over both sides of the fish; reserve the remaining paste mixture to serve. Wrap the fish in the banana leaves; secure with kitchen string or toothpicks.

4 Preheat a ridged cast-iron grill plate or barbecue to high heat. Cook the fish for 10 minutes on each side. Allow to stand for 5 minutes to finish cooking, before opening the leaves.

5 Meanwhile, to make the Thai herb salad, put the tomatoes, green onions, and herbs in a bowl. Combine the remaining ingredients in a small bowl. Just before serving, pour the dressing over the salad; toss to combine.

6 Open the banana-leaf parcel; discard the string or toothpicks. Serve the fish topped with the Thai herb salad and drizzled with the reserved red curry paste mixture.

TIPS

- If you can't source banana leaves, top 2 large sheets of foil with baking paper. Place the fish on 1 layered sheet of foil and top with the second stack, baking-paper-side down; fold in the edges several times to create a secure parcel.
- Prop up the fish tail with a ball of foil to prevent it burning on the barbecue or grill plate. The fish can be prepared to the end of step 3 up to 3 hours ahead; refrigerate until ready to cook.

Haloumi cheese skewers with blackberry dressing

GLUTEN-FREE | PREP + COOK TIME **30 MINUTES** | MAKES **8**

The semi-hard haloumi cheese has a high melting point, making it ideal for grilling.
It's important to thread same-sized pieces of the haloumi onto the same skewers, so that
all pieces of the haloumi touch the grill during cooking.

8 prosciutto slices (120g)

10 oz (350g) haloumi cheese,
cut into 24 pieces (see tips)

2 tbsp extra virgin olive oil

1 cup (25g) red endive, sliced

1 cup (25g) white endive, sliced

1/4 cup (35g) skinless toasted hazelnuts,
chopped

1/4 cup (7g) mint leaves

blackberry dressing

1/3 cup (95g) Greek-style yogurt

4 oz (125g) blackberries

1 tbsp sherry vinegar

1 tbsp honey

salt and freshly ground black pepper

1 To make the blackberry dressing, blend the ingredients in a blender or food processor until smooth and well combined; season with salt and pepper to taste.

2 Cut the prosciutto into 3 strips lengthwise. Roughly fold 8 strips of the prosciutto and thread onto 8 skewers. Thread a piece of haloumi cheese onto skewers; repeat twice with the remaining prosciutto and haloumi. Place the skewers on a plate; brush with the olive oil.

3 Meanwhile, preheat a ridged cast-iron grill pan or barbecue to high heat. Grill the skewers for 1 minute on each side or until the haloumi is well browned.

4 Arrange the endive and skewers on a plate; drizzle with the blackberry dressing. Serve with the hazelnuts and mint scattered over the top.

TIPS

- Endive is a bitter green. If you'd like a mellower flavor, try arugula or mixed salad greens instead.
- If you can't find fresh blackberries, thaw frozen blackberries and pat them dry before using.
- The dressing can be made up to 3 days ahead; refrigerate, covered, until needed.

Pork tenderloin with mushroom sauce

GLUTEN-FREE | PREP + COOK TIME **30 MINUTES** | SERVES **4**

Pork tenderloin, is one of the tenderest cuts of pork, as its name implies. That means it's highly suited to quick cooking methods. And for a speedy salad to accompany it, choose one of the Fast Salads on page 44.

16 fresh sage leaves

4 prosciutto slices (60g)

2 lbs (1 kg) pork tenderloin

2 tbsp olive oil

8 oz (225g) thinly sliced button mushrooms

1/4 cup (80g) thinly sliced onion

1 garlic clove, crushed

1 1/2 cups (375ml) gluten-free beef stock

1 tbsp tomato paste

1/4 lb (125g) frozen chopped spinach

1 lb (475g) premade gluten-free cheesy mashed potatoes

salt and freshly ground black pepper

1   Place 2 of the sage leaves along each slice of prosciutto. Wrap 2 slices of prosciutto around each pork tenderloin; secure in place with toothpicks or tie with kitchen string.

2   Preheat an oiled ridged cast-iron grill pan or barbecue to medium-high heat. Cook the pork, turning, for 10 minutes or until browned all over and cooked through. Remove from the pan; cover to keep warm.

3   Meanwhile, heat the olive oil in a medium frying pan over high heat. Cook the remaining sage leaves for 30 seconds or until crisp. Remove from the pan with a slotted spoon; set aside to drain on paper towels. Reduce the heat to medium-high. Cook the mushrooms, onion, and garlic in the same pan, stirring occasionally, for 4 minutes or until the mushrooms are golden and tender. Add the stock and tomato paste. Bring to a boil, then reduce the heat. Simmer for 5 minutes or until the sauce thickens slightly.

4   Meanwhile, microwave the spinach on HIGH (100%) for 1 minute or until hot. Place the spinach in a fine strainer; squeeze out the excess water. Heat the mashed potatoes according to the package directions. Transfer to a large serving bowl. Stir the spinach through the potatoes; season with salt and pepper to taste.

5   Thickly slice the pork; sprinkle with the crisp sage leaves. Serve with the mash and the mushroom sauce.

TIP

Pork is a lean cut, so care should be taken not to overcook it or it will be dry.

Thai fish burgers with pickled vegetables

CHEAT EAT | PREP + COOK TIME **30 MINUTES** | SERVES **4**

Pungently aromatic makrut lime leaves add their distinctive flavor to these fish burgers.
To use makrut lime leaves, fold a leaf in half and cut out the tough center vein. Leftover leaves
will keep in an airtight container in the fridge for 2 weeks or can be frozen for up to 1 month.

2 cucumbers (260g)

1 large carrot (180g)

2 long red chiles, thinly sliced

2 tbsp sugar

2 tbsp white vinegar

1¼ lb (600g) skinless white fish fillets

2 tbsp Thai red curry paste

2 tbsp fish sauce

4 fresh makrut lime leaves, thinly sliced

6 green beans, thinly sliced

1 egg

½ cup (15g) cilantro

2 tbsp peanut or vegetable oil

⅓ cup (80ml) sweet chili sauce

4 brioche buns, split horizontally

1 Using a mandoline, V-slicer, or wide vegetable peeler, thinly slice the cucumber and carrot lengthwise into long ribbons. Combine the cucumber, carrot, chiles, sugar, and white vinegar in a medium bowl. Allow to stand for 10 minutes or until the vegetables have softened, turning every few minutes. Drain.

2 Meanwhile, in a food processor, pulse the fish, red curry paste, fish sauce, lime leaves, green beans, egg, and half of the cilantro leaves for 1 minute or until smooth. Using oiled hands, shape the mixture into four 5 in patties.

3 Heat the peanut oil in a large frying pan over medium heat. Cook the patties for 2 minutes on each side or until cooked through. Drain on paper towels.

4 Add the brioche buns, cut-side down, to the same frying pan; cook for 1 minute or until lightly toasted.

5 Sandwich the fish burgers, sweet chili sauce, pickled vegetables, and remaining cilantro in the rolls. Serve immediately.

TIP

Fish patties can be prepared several hours ahead; store, covered, in the fridge until ready to cook.

Bangers and mash dinner

KID-FRIENDLY | PREP + COOK TIME **30 MINUTES** | SERVES **4**

Bangers and mash are a classic pub dinner and make a hearty weeknight option. For this easy supper, look for lamb sausages to pair with the traditional mint sauce. Try with artisanal sausages from your favorite butcher.

2¼ lbs (1.2 kg) lamb sausages (see tips)

1¾ lbs (800g) all-purpose potatoes, peeled, coarsely chopped

1 lb (500g) frozen fava beans

1 lb (400g) heirloom carrots, trimmed

3 tbsp (40g) butter

½ cup (125ml) hot milk

¼ cup (7g) mint leaves

salt and freshly ground black pepper

mint sauce

2 cups (50g) firmly packed mint leaves

2 garlic cloves, quartered

½ cup (125ml) olive oil

¼ cup (60ml) white wine vinegar

1 tbsp sugar

1 Heat a ridged cast-iron grill pan (or grill) over medium-high heat. Cook the sausages, turning, for 8 minutes or until cooked through.

2 Meanwhile, boil, steam, or microwave the potatoes, beans, and carrots separately until tender; drain. Cover the carrots to keep warm. Push the potatoes through a fine strainer into a large bowl; stir in the butter and milk until smooth. Peel the fava beans. Put the beans in a small bowl; crush coarsely with fork. Fold the beans into the potato mixture. Season with salt and pepper to taste; cover to keep warm.

3 To make the mint sauce, blend or process the mint and garlic until smooth. With the motor operating, gradually add the oil, in a thin, steady stream, until the mixture is smooth. Stir in the vinegar and sugar.

4 Serve the sausages with the mint sauce, carrots, and broad bean mash, sprinkled with the mint leaves. Season with salt and pepper to taste.

TIPS

- If you can't find lamb sausages, substitute bratwurst or pork sausages instead.
- Use frozen peas instead of fava beans, if you like.

Sausage and peppers with soft polenta

KID-FRIENDLY | PREP + COOK TIME **30 MINUTES** | SERVES **4**

This is quick winter comfort food at its best and can be made even faster if you would like by swapping out the polenta for prepackaged cheesy mashed potatoes. The creamy polenta is well worth the small amount of effort required, though, and the reward is in its eating.

2 tbsp olive oil

1 lb (500g) pork and fennel sausages

1¹/₂ lbs (700g) red bell peppers, seeded, thickly sliced

1¹/₂ cups (400g) thinly sliced onion

2 tbsp rosemary

3 garlic cloves, sliced

1 cup (250ml) dry white wine

6 cups (1.5 liters) chicken stock

¹/₂ lb (250g) green beans, trimmed

1 cup (170g) polenta

1 cup (100g) finely grated Parmesan cheese, plus extra 2 tbsp

2 tbsp (30g) butter, chopped

salt and freshly ground black pepper

1   Heat the olive oil in a large, heavy-based skillet over high heat. Squeeze the sausage meat directly from the casings, in meatball-sized lumps, into the pan. Cook, turning, for 4 minutes or until browned. Remove the sausage from the pan; set aside to drain on a paper-towel-lined plate.

2   Reduce the heat to medium. Cook the red peppers, onions, rosemary, and garlic for 5 minutes. Add the sausage and wine; cook for 1 minute. Add 1 cup (250ml) of the stock and the green beans to the pan; cook, covered, for 10 minutes or until the sausage is cooked through.

3   Meanwhile, put the remaining 5 cups (1.25 liters) stock in a medium saucepan; bring to a boil. Gradually add the polenta. Reduce the heat to low; cook, stirring, for 5 minutes or until thickened. Remove from the heat, and stir in the 1 cup (80g) Parmesan cheese and the butter; season with salt and pepper to taste.

4   Serve the meatballs with the polenta and green beans, sprinkled with the extra Parmesan cheese.

Salmon with fennel and ruby grapefruit salad

HEALTHY CHOICE | PREP + COOK TIME **30 MINUTES** | SERVES **4**

You can also use a white fish such as mackerel or sea bass for this recipe. The salad, with its balance of bold flavors and textures, acts as a foil to the succulent fish. When segmenting the grapefruit, don't forget to reserve 2 tablespoons of the juice to use in the dressing.

³/₄ lb (400g) fennel bulbs, thinly sliced, fronds reserved

1¹/₂ lbs (700g) ruby red grapefruit, peeled and segmented, with 2 tbsp juice reserved for the dressing

8 oz (225g) radishes, trimmed, thinly sliced (see tips)

¹/₄ cup (80g) thinly sliced red onions

³/₄ cup (120g) kalamata olives

¹/₄ cup (7g) firmly packed flat-leaf parsley leaves

¹/₄ cup (7g) firmly packed mint

1 tbsp lemon juice

2 tbsp extra virgin olive oil, divided

4 x ¹/₂ lb (800g) salmon fillets, skin on

2 tbsp (30g) butter

salt and freshly ground black pepper

citrus dressing

2 tbsp extra virgin olive oil

2 tbsp reserved red grapefruit juice (see above)

1 tbsp lemon juice

1 tsp Dijon mustard

1　To make the citrus dressing, put the ingredients in a small screw-top jar with a tight-fitting lid; shake until well combined. Season with salt and pepper to taste. Set aside.

2　Put the fennel, grapefruit, radishes, onion, olives, parsley, and mint in a large bowl with the lemon juice and 1 tablespoon of the olive oil; toss gently to combine. Season with salt and pepper to taste.

3　Heat the remaining 1 tablespoon olive oil in a large heavy-based frying pan over high heat. Season the salmon with salt and pepper to taste. Cook the salmon, skin-side down, for 1 minute or until golden brown. Turn over; add the butter to the pan. Cook until the butter turns nut brown. Continue cooking the salmon for a further 30 seconds or until just cooked through.

4　Divide the salad and salmon evenly among 4 serving plates; sprinkle with the reserved fennel fronds. Season with salt and pepper to taste. Drizzle with the citrus dressing, and serve.

TIPS

- Use a mandoline or V-slicer, if you have one, to thinly slice the fennel, radishes, and onion.
- The dressing can be made and refrigerated in the jar up to 2 days ahead.

Greek pork skewers with crushed white beans

KID-FRIENDLY | PREP + COOK TIME **30 MINUTES** | SERVES **4**

Souvlaki, skewers of grilled meat and sometimes vegetables usually cooked over a spit, is almost an art form in Greece and a very popular street food. The usual choice of meat is pork, as in the skewers here, and they are accompanied by another Greek standard, a chunky white bean dip made with cannellini or white kidney beans.

$1/4$ cup (60ml) extra virgin olive oil, divided

$1/2$ cup (150g) thinly sliced onion

3 garlic cloves, 1 thinly sliced and 2 halved

$1/2$ cup (125ml) dry white wine

2 x 15.5 oz (439g) cans cannellini beans, drained, rinsed

1 cup (250ml) chicken stock

2 tbsp lemon juice

2 tbsp coarsely chopped oregano, plus extra 2–3 tbsp

1 tsp finely grated lemon zest

2 tbsp red wine vinegar

$1^{1}/2$ lb (700g) pork tenderloin, diced into 1-in pieces

2 tbsp flat-leaf parsley

strips of lemon zest (or use 2 tsp grated zest)

salt and freshly ground black pepper

lemon wedges, to serve

1. Heat 1 tablespoon of the olive oil in a saucepan over medium heat. Add the onion and thinly sliced garlic to the pan; cook, stirring, for 6 minutes or until tender. Add the wine, stirring to combine, then add the cannellini beans and stock. Bring to a simmer; cook, stirring occasionally, for 15 minutes or until thickened. Crush the beans with a fork; stir in the lemon juice and the 2 tablespoons chopped oregano. Season with salt and pepper to taste. Cover and set aside to keep warm.

2. Meanwhile, process the remaining olive oil, lemon zest, garlic halves, red wine vinegar, and extra $2^{1}/2$ tablespoons oregano until the mixture forms a paste; season with salt and pepper to taste. Combine the oregano mixture and the pork in a medium bowl; thread the pork onto skewers.

3. Preheat a ridged cast-iron grill pan (or grill or barbecue) to medium heat. Cook the skewers, turning occasionally, for 6 minutes or until cooked through. Serve accompanied by the crushed white beans sprinkled with the parsley and strips of lemon zest, with lemon wedges for squeezing over.

TIP

If cooking the pork skewers in a ridged cast-iron grill pan, you won't need to soak the bamboo skewers first. However, if you are grilling with a live flame, you will need to do this, to prevent them from scorching or burning while cooking. Place the bamboo skewers in a heatproof bowl, fill with boiling water, and soak for 5 minutes; drain.

Fast pizza

When everyone comes home hungry and in a rush, or unexpected guests arrive at the door and you need to whip up a meal, reach for one—or more!—of these pizza ideas as the perfect solution. Indeed, you can use them any time the yen for a pizza is calling.

Salami, ricotta, and kale

PREP TIME + COOK TIME **15 MINUTES** | SERVES **4**

Oil 2 baking sheets or pizza pans; place in the oven, then preheat to 475°F. On floured parchment paper, roll two 8 oz (225g) ready-made dough balls into two 6in x 12in ovals. Transfer to the baking sheets on the parchment paper; spread with $1/3$ cup (80ml) pizza or pasta sauce (with herbs and garlic). Top with 5 oz (150g) pepperoni or other salami, 1 lb (500g) cherry vine tomatoes, $1/4$ cup (80g) thinly sliced small red onion, and $1/2$ cup (130g) crumbled fresh ricotta cheese; bake for 15 minutes or until the bases are browned and crisp. Serve topped with 1 cup (60g) fresh baby greens.

Teriyaki chicken and pineapple

PREP TIME + COOK TIME **15 MINUTES** | SERVES **4**

Oil 2 baking sheets or pizza pans; place in the oven, then preheat to 475°F. On floured parchment paper, roll two 8 oz (225g) ready-made dough balls into two 6in x 12in ovals. Transfer to the baking sheets on the parchment paper. Drain an 8 oz (227g) can pineapple pieces; drain again on paper towels. Combine $1/3$ cup (80ml) barbecue sauce with 2 tablespoons teriyaki sauce in a small bowl. Spread two-thirds of the sauce mixture onto the bases; top with $1^1/2$ cups (260g) shredded grilled or rotisserie chicken, 1 thinly sliced red bell pepper, 1 thinly sliced portabella mushroom cap, and the drained pineapple. Bake the pizzas for 15 minutes or until the bases are browned and crisp. Serve drizzled with the remaining sauce mixture and sprinkled with 2 thinly sliced green onions.

Tomato and mozzarella

PREP TIME + COOK TIME **15 MINUTES** | SERVES **4**

Oil 2 baking sheets or pizza pans; place in the oven, then preheat to 475°F. On floured parchment paper, roll two 8 oz (225g) ready-made dough balls into two 15cm x 30cm ovals. Transfer to the baking sheets on the parchment paper; spread with $1/2$ cup (125ml) pizza or pasta sauce. Top with $3/4$ lb (400g) thickly sliced mixed baby heirloom tomatoes and 5 oz (150g) torn buffalo mozzarella. Bake the pizzas for 15 minutes or until the bases are browned and crisp. Drizzle with 1 tablespoon olive oil and 2 teaspoons balsamic vinegar. Sprinkle with 1 tablespoon roasted pine nuts, $1/4$ cup (15g) small fresh basil leaves, and $1/4$ cup (25g) shaved Parmesan cheese.

Sweet potato and rosemary

PREP TIME + COOK TIME **15 MINUTES** | SERVES **4**

Oil 2 baking sheets or pizza pans; place in the oven, then preheat to 475°F. On floured parchment paper, roll two 8 oz (225g) ready-made dough balls into two 6in x 12in ovals. Transfer to the baking sheets on the parchment paper; spread with combined $1/3$ cup (80ml) olive oil, 1 crushed garlic clove, and 1 tablespoon chopped rosemary. Using a vegetable peeler, mandoline, or V-slicer, slice 1 small sweet potato into paper-thin strips. Sprinkle with 4 oz (100g) crumbled feta cheese. Bake the pizzas for 15 minutes or until the bases are browned and crisp. Serve topped with 1 cup (50g) arugula leaves and drizzled with 1 tablespoon olive oil.

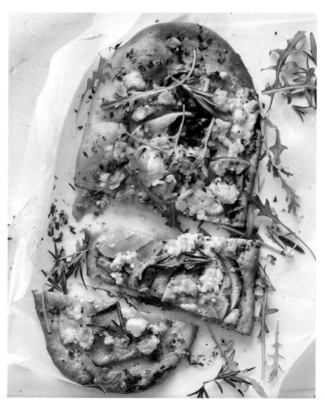

Mushroom and goat cheese ravioli with brown butter

MEAT-FREE | PREP + COOK TIME **30 MINUTES + STANDING & COOLING** | SERVES **4**

Gyoza or potsticker wrappers are a quick shortcut to fresh pasta when it comes to making these ravioli. The brown butter sauce is made by gently cooking butter to the point where the milk solids separate from the fat and are transformed into a toasty, sweet-flavored mixture.

8 oz (225g) button mushrooms

4 oz (100g) marinated goat cheese, oil reserved

$\frac{1}{4}$ cup (7g) tarragon leaves, plus extra, to serve

24 gyoza wrappers

5 tbsp (75g) butter

$\frac{1}{4}$ cup (25g) walnuts, coarsely chopped, plus extra, to serve

salt and freshly ground black pepper

1 Finely chop the mushrooms. Heat 1 tablespoon of the reserved oil from the marinated goat cheese in a medium skillet over medium-high heat; cook the mushrooms, stirring, for 4 minutes or until soft. Season with salt and pepper to taste. Transfer to a heatproof bowl; allow to cool to room temperature. Reserve the skillet, without rinsing.

2 Finely chop 2 tablespoons of the tarragon. Add the chopped tarragon and goat cheese to the cooled mushroom mixture; stir to combine.

3 Place 12 gyoza or potsticker wrappers on a clean work surface. Spoon the filling onto the center of each wrapper. Dampen around the edge of each wrapper with a little water; top with the remaining wrappers, pressing together the edges to seal.

4 Cook the ravioli in a large saucepan of boiling salted water, in batches, for 2 minutes or until they float to the surface. Remove the ravioli with a slotted spoon; place in a single layer on a baking sheet. Cover to keep warm.

5 Melt the butter in the reserved frying pan over low heat. Add the walnuts and remaining tarragon; cook gently until the butter begins to turn a nutty brown color. Add the cooked ravioli to the pan; toss gently to coat. Remove the pan from the heat.

6 Serve the ravioli topped with extra tarragon leaves and extra walnuts. Season with pepper to taste.

TIP

If you can't find gyoza or potsticker wrappers, you can use square wonton wrappers or other dumpling wrappers instead.

Steak and potatoes with salsa verde

GLUTEN-FREE | PREP + COOK TIME **30 MINUTES** | SERVES **4**

Salsa verde, the ubiquitous Italian green sauce, livens up most things. Variations of salsa verde are found in Spanish and French cooking, too. If you have sauce left over, slather it on the inside of a roll to elevate a sandwich or drizzle over veggies to add a burst of flavor.

1 tbsp olive oil

4 tbsp (60g) butter

1 lb (500g) fingerling potatoes, halved lengthwise

1³/₄ lb (800g) beef tenderloin, sliced into 8 medallions

10 oz (350g), arugula (see tip)

salt and freshly ground black pepper

salsa verde

1 garlic clove, crushed

1 tsp Dijon mustard

2 tsp capers

2 anchovy fillets

3 tsp red wine vinegar

3 cornichons

¹/₄ cup (5g) mint leaves

¹/₄ cup (7g) basil leaves

2 tbsp coarsely chopped flat-leaf parsley

¹/₄ cup (60ml) olive oil

1 Preheat the oven to 425°F.

2 Toss the potatoes with the olive oil on the baking sheet; season with salt and pepper to taste. Roast the potatoes for 20 minutes or until golden and tender.

3 Melt the butter over medium-high heat in a large cast iron skillet; cook the beef for 2¹/₂ minutes on each side for medium, basting with the butter, or until cooked to your liking. Remove the meat from the pan to let rest. Keep warm while making the sauce.

4 To make the salsa verde, combine the ingredients in the bowl of a food processor until finely chopped; season with salt and pepper to taste.

5 Serve the steak with the potatoes, watercress, and salsa verde.

TIP

To save time, you can find prewashed and trimmed arugula or mixed greens in the refrigerated salad section of your local grocery store.

Spanish chicken, chorizo, and rice soup

CHEAP EAT | PREP + COOK TIME **30 MINUTES** | SERVES **4**

Comfort in a bowl, this hearty dish is a soupier version of the classic Spanish chicken and rice. If you'd like to ramp up the flavors in the soup even further, swap the sweet paprika for Spanish smoked paprika and add a pinch of dried red chili flakes.

2 tbsp (30g) butter

¼ cup (80g) finely chopped onion

2 garlic cloves, crushed

1 large red bell pepper (200g), finely chopped

2 tsp dried oregano

1 tsp sweet paprika

1 tsp ground cumin

1 tbsp all-purpose flour

2 tbsp tomato paste

4 cups (1 liter) chicken stock

1 x 14 oz can (397g) crushed tomatoes

½ cup (100g) uncooked medium-grain rice

6 oz (170g) Spanish chorizo, thinly sliced

2 cups (320g) shredded cooked chicken

2 avocados (300g)

½ cup (25g) coarsely chopped cilantro

salt and freshly ground black pepper

2 limes, halved, to serve

1 Melt the butter in a large saucepan over medium heat; cook the onion and garlic, stirring, for 5 minutes or until the onion softens. Add the red pepper, oregano, paprika, and ground cumin; cook, stirring, until fragrant. Add the flour and tomato paste; cook, stirring, for 1 minute. Gradually stir in the stock, 2 cups (500ml) water, and the crushed tomatoes; bring to a boil, stirring. Stir in the rice; simmer uncovered, stirring occasionally, for 15 minutes or until the rice is tender.

2 Meanwhile, heat a large oiled frying pan over medium-high heat. Cook the chorizo until browned. Drain on paper towels.

3 Add the chorizo and chicken to the soup; stir over medium heat until hot. Season with salt and pepper to taste. Slice the avocado, remove the pits, and carefully scoop each half from the shell. Chop the avocado halves.

4 Serve bowls of the soup topped with the avocado and cilantro, and accompanied by the lime halves for squeezing over.

Veal scaloppine with lemon and capers

GLUTEN-FREE | PREP + COOK TIME **30 MINUTES** | SERVES **6**

Veal scaloppine, veal cutlets, veal schnitzel—they are one and the same. These thinly sliced pieces of veal are perfect for breading. Just place between two sheets of parchment paper and pound them flat if needed. Serve with mashed potato instead of polenta, if you like.

1 cup (170g) quick-cook polenta

³/₄ cup (180ml) milk

¹/₄ cup (25g) finely grated Parmesan cheese

1 tbsp cracked black pepper

1¹/₄ lb (600g) veal cutlets (at least 6)

4 tbsp (60g) butter

1 tbsp drained capers, rinsed

3 strips of lemon zest, thinly sliced

¹/₃ cup (80ml) lemon juice

2 tbsp parsley

salt and freshly ground black pepper

1 Bring 2 cups (500ml) water to a boil in a medium saucepan. Stir in the polenta, and reduce the heat to low. Cook, stirring, for 5 minutes or until the polenta thickens. Stir in the milk; cook, still stirring, for 5 minutes or until the polenta thickens. Stir in the Parmesan cheese; season with salt and pepper to taste. Keep warm until needed.

2 Meanwhile, sprinkle the 1 tablespoon cracked black pepper over both sides of the veal. Heat the butter in a large frying pan over medium-high heat; cook the veal, in batches, for 2–3 minutes on each side or until lightly browned. Remove from the pan; cover and set aside to keep warm.

3 Add the capers, lemon zest, lemon juice, and 1 tablespoon water to the same pan; bring to a boil, stirring. Spoon the sauce over the veal, and sprinkle with the parsley. Serve the polenta with the veal.

TIP

Serve with steamed green beans and sprinkle the polenta with extra grated Parmesan cheese, if you like.

Couscous and dill-crusted fish

HEALTHY CHOICE | PREP + COOK TIME **20 MINUTES** | SERVES **4**

This recipe showcases a clever way to use couscous, flavored with fresh dill and garlic, as a crunchy coating on the fish. Oven-baking rather than pan-frying the fish takes it all one step further, to keep things healthy.

$\frac{1}{2}$ cup (100g) instant couscous

4 tbsp coarsely chopped dill

2 garlic cloves, crushed

2 tbsp extra virgin olive oil

1$\frac{3}{4}$ lb (800g) skinless firm white fish fillets

$\frac{1}{3}$ lb (175g) broccolini,
thickly sliced on the diagonal

2 cups (240g) frozen peas

1 cup (280g) Greek-style yogurt

2 tbsp tahini

1 tbsp lemon juice

$\frac{1}{3}$ cup (25g) flaked almonds, toasted

salt and freshly ground black pepper

lemon wedges, to serve

1 Preheat the oven to 425°F. Line a large baking sheet with parchment paper.

2 Put the couscous, 2 tablespoons of the chopped dill, half of the crushed garlic, $\frac{1}{2}$ cup (125ml) water, and the olive oil in a small bowl. Using your fingertips, rub the couscous grains until evenly covered with the mixture; season with salt and pepper to taste. Place the fish on the prepared baking sheet; press the couscous mixture onto the fish. Bake for 12 minutes or until the fish is cooked through and the crust is golden.

3 Meanwhile, cook the broccolini in a saucepan of boiling water for 2 minutes. Add the peas; cook for a further minute or until the vegetables are tender; drain.

4 Combine the yogurt, tahini, lemon juice, and remaining crushed garlic in a small bowl; season with salt and pepper to taste. Spoon the yogurt mixture onto 4 plates. Top with the vegetables, fish, almonds, and remaining 2 tablespoons chopped dill. Serve with the lemon wedges for squeezing over.

TIP

You could also try this recipe with skinless salmon fillets replacing the white fish fillets.

Shrimp with orzo and peas

KID-FRIENDLY | PREP + COOK TIME **20 MINUTES** | SERVES **2**

Garlicky shrimp and fresh peas combine here to make a light but satisfying meal perfect for summer evenings. You could make the recipe using clams instead of shrimp and pearl couscous instead of orzo. The recipe can easily be doubled to serve four.

2 tbsp (30g) butter, chopped

2 garlic cloves, crushed, divided

$1/2$ cup (125ml) chicken stock

$2^1/2$ cups (300g) frozen peas

1 cup (220g) dried orzo

4 tbsp extra virgin olive oil, divided

1 lb (540g) uncooked medium shrimp, peeled, tails intact

$1/4$ cup (7g) coarsely chopped flat-leaf parsley

1 long red chile, seeded, finely chopped

salt and freshly ground black pepper

lemon wedges, to serve

1 Heat the butter in a small saucepan over low heat. Once foaming, add one clove of the garlic; cook, stirring, until lightly golden. Add the stock and $1/2$ cup (125ml) water. Bring to a boil, then reduce the heat slightly. Add the peas; cook, covered, for 3 minutes or until tender. Remove and reserve $1/2$ cup (60g) of the peas. Set aside.

2 Cook the orzo in a saucepan of boiling water until almost tender; drain.

3 Meanwhile, heat 2 tablespoons of the olive oil in a large frying pan over high heat. Cook the shrimp for 1 minute. Add the remaining garlic, then turn the shrimp over. Cook for a further minute or until changed in color and just cooked through.

4 Using a hand-held blender (or small food processor), coarsely purée the pea and stock mixture; stir in the reserved whole peas. Season with salt and pepper to taste. Add the purée mixture and orzo to the pan with the shrimp; stir to combine. Cook for a further minute or until heated through. Stir in the parsley and chile.

5 To serve, divide the mixture between 2 bowls. Drizzle with the remaining 2 tablespoons olive oil. Serve accompanied by the lemon wedges for squeezing over.

TIP

Orzo, which means "barley" in Italian, is a rice-shaped pasta often used in soups such as minestrone.

Steamed fish with tahini yogurt

HEALTHY CHOICE | PREP + COOK TIME **25 MINUTES** | SERVES **4**

This delicious and healthy pairing of fish with tahini yogurt is a popular combination throughout the Middle East, and especially in Lebanon where it is a coastal specialty and usually features baked fish and pine nuts. Almonds are used here instead.

1³/₄ lb (800g) skinless firm white fish fillets

¹/₃ cup (80ml) lemon juice

³/₄ lb (360g) zucchini, trimmed, sliced lengthwise into ribbons

½ lb (280g) radishes, trimmed, thinly sliced

1 tbsp tahini

¹/₃ cup (95g) Greek-style yogurt

¹/₄ cup (10g) finely chopped cilantro, plus extra ¹/₄ cup (7g) for serving

½ cup (70g) roasted slivered almonds

¹/₄ tsp dried chili flakes

¹/₄ cup (60ml) extra virgin olive oil, divided

salt and freshly ground black pepper

1 Put the fish in a steamer lined with parchment paper. Place the steamer over a saucepan of simmering water. Cook, covered, for 8 minutes or until the fish is just cooked through.

2 Meanwhile, combine the lemon juice, zucchini, and radishes in a small bowl; allow to stand until the vegetables are pickled, or until needed.

3 Combine the tahini and yogurt in a small bowl; season with salt and pepper to taste. Combine the ¹/₄ cup (7g) chopped cilantro, almonds, chili flakes, and 2 tablespoons of the olive oil in another small bowl.

4 Carefully transfer the fish from the steamer to a plate. Cover each portion generously with the tahini yogurt mixture, then top with the cilantro mixture.

5 Add the remaining olive oil to the bowl with the zucchini and radishes, season with salt and pepper to taste; toss to combine.

6 Serve the fish with the pickled vegetables, with the extra cilantro leaves sprinkled over the top. Accompany with couscous or flatbread, if you like.

TIPS

- You could make the recipe using salmon, if you like.
- Try replacing the zucchini with a shaved bulb of baby fennel.
- Use a mandoline or V-slicer to thinly slice the radishes and zucchini.

Pork parmigiana bake

KID-FRIENDLY | PREP + COOK TIME **25 MINUTES** | SERVES **4**

This delectable dish of layered tastes and textures has echoes of the Italian-American comfort-food classic. It can be served as is, or accompany it with a salad—or even mashed potato and fresh crusty bread, to soak up the juices.

1 small eggplant (230g), thinly sliced lengthwise

olive oil cooking spray

4 prosciutto slices (60g)

2 tbsp olive oil, divided

4 uncrumbed pork escalopes (400g)

4 mozzarella balls (240g)

2 tbsp finely grated Parmesan cheese

400g can cherry tomatoes

1/3 cup (7g) basil leaves

salt and freshly ground black pepper

1 Preheat a ridged cast-iron grill pan or barbecue to high heat. Spray the eggplant on both sides with the cooking spray. Cook for 2 minutes on each side or until browned and tender. Set aside.

2 Meanwhile, preheat the broiler to high heat. Arrange the prosciutto on a baking sheet lined with foil; place under the broiler. Broil for 3 minutes or until the prosciutto is browned and crisp. Remove from the oven; cover and set aside to keep warm. Do not turn off the oven.

3 Meanwhile, heat 1 tablespoon of the olive oil in a shallow 2-liter (8-cup) flameproof baking dish over medium-high heat on the hob. Season the pork with salt and pepper to taste; cook for 1 minute on each side or until almost cooked through; remove from the heat. Remove the pork from the dish. Set aside on a plate to keep warm.

4 Slice the mozzarella balls thinly. Add the tomatoes to the baking dish. Arrange the pork on top, then top the pork with the sliced eggplant, mozzarella, and Parmesan cheese.

5 Place the baking dish under the hot broiler; cook for 3 minutes or until the bocconcini melts and the pork is cooked through.

6 To serve, spoon the tomato over the pork. Top with the prosciutto and cress. Drizzle with the remaining 1 tablespoon olive oil, and serve.

TIP

Put the baking dish as close to the preheated broiler as possible.

DESSERTS

Choose from an array of treats to satisfy dessert cravings—from melting meringues to oozy puddings, fresh fruit sensations to new twists on classic favorites.

Sumac strawberry pavlovas

GLUTEN-FREE | PREP + COOK TIME **10 MINUTES + REFRIGERATION** | SERVES **4**

Sumac is a purple-red, tangy spice, ground from berries growing on shrubs that flourish in the wild around the Mediterranean. Here, the sumac adds a tart, lemony flavor that contrasts well with the sweetness of the meringue.

8 oz (225g) strawberries,
thinly sliced into rounds (see tips)

1/3 cup (55g) powdered sugar, sifted

1 tbsp sumac

1 1/4 cups (300ml) whipping cream

1 tsp pure vanilla extract

8 oz premade meringue cookies (240g)

1 Combine the strawberries, sifted powdered sugar, and sumac in a small bowl. Cover; refrigerate for 30 minutes.

2 Just before serving, beat together the cream and vanilla in a small bowl using an electric mixer until firm peaks form. Spoon the cream equally among the meringue cookies, then top with the sumac strawberries. Serve immediately.

TIPS

- Don't slice the strawberries too thinly, or they will fall apart during refrigeration.
- Premade plain meringues are a gluten-free product, but always check the label first, to make sure there are no hidden extras.

Lamington cream layer cake

KID-FRIENDLY | PREP + COOK TIME **30 MINUTES** | SERVES **8**

The lamington was originally created by a cook as a way of refreshing sponge cake. Debate swirls around what makes a "proper" lamington, with some devotees firmly in the no-jam-or-cream camp, but all agree on the soaking of chocolate frosting with a coconut coating.

1¼ cups (300ml) whipping cream

2 chocolate fudge or devil's food cake rounds from 1 package of boxed mix or your favorite recipe (see tips)

½ cup (160g) strawberry jam

1 16oz (453g) can milk chocolate or dark chocolate frosting

1½ cups (120g) shredded coconut

1   Using an electric mixer, beat the cream in a small bowl until firm peaks form.

2   Split the cake rounds in half. Place a cake layer on a board; spread with 2 tablespoons of the jam. Top with one-third of the cream, leaving a ½ inch border around the edge; top with another cake layer. Repeat the layering with the remaining jam, cream, and cake layers, finishing with a cake layer.

3   Spread the side of the cake with three-quarters of the chocolate frosting. Gently press the coconut to the sides of the cake until the sides are covered.

4   Spread the remaining frosting over the top of the cake, then gently press the remaining coconut all over the top of the cake.

TIPS

- You can make the cake rounds ahead of time. Simply follow the package directions, cool the rounds, then wrap tightly in plastic wrap and refrigerate overnight. Or you can use your favorite cake recipe.
- If you'd prefer, you can make this cake with white or yellow cake.

Salted caramel and apple ice-cream sundaes

KID-FRIENDLY | PREP + COOK TIME **10 MINUTES** | SERVES **4**

These sundaes seem like autumnal decadence in a glass—but you can enjoy them at any time of the year. You could use pears instead of apples. Make sure to choose a firm variety of pear that holds its shape during cooking, such as Packham or Beurre Bosc.

5 tbsp (70g) butter, chopped

³/₄ lb (400g) honeycrisp or golden delicious apples, peeled, cored, coarsely chopped

1 tbsp lemon juice

¹/₂ cup (75g) light brown sugar

¹/₄ tsp cinnamon

¹/₈ tsp allspice

¹/₈ tsp nutmeg

¹/₄ tsp sea salt flakes

¹/₄ cup (60ml) whipping cream

8 scoops of good-quality vanilla ice cream

4 amaretti cookies, crumbled

¹/₄ cup (40g) toasted pine nuts

1 Melt the butter in a large sauté pan over medium heat. Add the apples and lemon juice; cook for 5 minutes. Add the brown sugar, cinnamon, allspice, nutmeg, sea salt, and cream; cook, stirring, for 1 minute.

2 Divide the ice cream among 4 glasses. Spoon over the warm apple mixture; sprinkle with the crumbled cookies and pine nuts. Serve the sundaes immediately.

TIP

To create more flavor variations of this recipe, use a different-flavored ice cream or nuts such as pecans or hazelnuts.

Fast ice-cream sandwiches

The only thing speedier than preparing these ice-cream sandwiches is how fast they will be devoured. Serve them for a children's party or for adults who are big kids themselves. They also work well for casual entertaining because they are the dessert equivalent of finger food.

Pretzel caramel

PREP TIME **20 MINUTES + FREEZING** | MAKES **4**

Place 4 cookies with chocolate icing, chocolate side down on a cutting board. Working with one at a time, top each cookie with a small scoop of salted caramel or coffee ice cream, then sandwich with another cookie icing side up. Place on a sheet lined with plastic wrap; freeze for 10 minutes. Place 1 cup of salted pretzels in a plastic zip-top bag; pound with a rolling pin until coarsely crushed. Place in a shallow bowl. Working with one at a time, unwrap the ice-cream sandwiches, and roll the sides in the crushed pretzels. Serve immediately or freeze until needed.

Fruity fizz

PREP TIME **20 MINUTES + FREEZING** | MAKES **4**

Place 4 crispy sugar cookies with pink icing, icing-side down on a cutting board. Working with one at a time, top each cookie with a scoop of cherry swirl ice cream, then sandwich with another sugar cookie, icing-side up. Place on a sheet lined with plastic wrap, wrap tightly; freeze for 10 minutes. Place a small package of sweet-tart candies in a plastic zip-top bag; pound with a rolling pin until coarsely crushed. Place in a shallow bowl. Again working with one at a time, unwrap the ice-cream sandwiches, and roll the sides in the crushed candies. Serve immediately or freeze until needed.

Loaded triple choc

PREP TIME **20 MINUTES + FREEZING** | MAKES **4**

Place 4 chocolate chip cookies, rounded-side down, on a cutting board. Working with one at a time, top each cookie with a scoop of chocolate ice cream, then sandwich with another chocolate chip cookie, rounded-side up. Place on a sheet lined with plastic wrap, wrap tightly, and freeze. Place $1/2$ cup of mini candy-coated chocolates in a shallow bowl. Again working with one at a time, unwrap the ice-cream sandwiches, and roll the sides in the chocolates. Serve immediately or freeze until needed.

Minty crisp

PREP TIME **20 MINUTES + FREEZING** | MAKES **4**

Place 4 mint fudge cookies, rounded-side down, on a board. Working with one at a time, top each cookie with a scoop of mint chocolate chip ice cream, then sandwich with another mint fudge cookie, rounded-side up. Place on a sheet lined with plastic wrap; freeze for 10 minutes. Finely chop 2 peppermint crisp or other peppermint chocolate bars; place in a shallow bowl. Again working with one at a time, unwrap the ice-cream sandwiches, and roll the sides in the crushed peppermint crisp. Serve immediately or freeze until needed.

Charred peaches with berry rosewater yogurt

GLUTEN-FREE | PREP + COOK TIME **15 MINUTES** | SERVES **4**

Ripe, juicy stone fruits are often best treated simply, so that their sweet, subtle flavors become the stars of the show. For a nut-free version, replace the pistachios with toasted shredded coconut or pumpkin seeds, or omit them altogether; it will be equally delicious.

2 lbs (1 kg) peaches, halved, pits removed

2 tbsp coarsely chopped pistachios

berry rosewater yogurt

5 oz (150g) strawberries, sliced

1 tbsp rosewater

1 cup (280g) gluten-free vanilla yogurt

1 To make the berry rosewater yogurt, blend or process the strawberries with the rosewater until smooth. Swirl through the yogurt.

2 Preheat an oiled ridged cast-iron grill pan or barbecue to medium-high heat. Grill the peaches, cut-side down, for 5 minutes or until charred and tender.

3 Divide the peaches among 4 serving plates. Spoon the berry rosewater yogurt over the peaches. Serve with the chopped pistachios sprinkled over the top.

TIP

You can use thawed frozen strawberries or raspberries for this recipe, and either white or yellow peaches. If peaches are unavailable, mango cheeks, pineapple wedges, small ripe pear halves, or thick apple slices make good alternatives.

Waffles à la Suzette

KID-FRIENDLY | PREP + COOK TIME **20 MINUTES** | SERVES **4**

Traditionally Suzette sauce, a wonderful alchemy of caramelized sugar, butter, orange juice, and orange liqueur, accompanies crêpes. Waffles replace crêpes in our recipe to create an instant dessert, minus the flambée.

1 stick 8 tbsp (125g) butter, chopped

½ cup (110g) sugar

2 tsp finely grated orange zest

½ cup (125ml) orange juice

8 Belgian-style waffles (480g)

2 medium oranges (480g), peeled, thinly sliced into rounds

2 cups (500ml) vanilla ice cream

2 tbsp toasted flaked almonds

1 To make the Suzette sauce, melt the butter in a small heavy-based saucepan. Add the sugar, orange zest, and orange juice; cook, stirring, over low heat and without boiling, until the sugar dissolves. Bring to a boil. Reduce the heat; simmer, without stirring, for 2 minutes or until the sauce thickens slightly.

2 Heat the waffles according to the package instructions.

3 Divide the waffles and orange slices among 4 serving plates. Top with scoops of the ice cream, Suzette sauce, and a scattering of almonds.

TIP

If you would like to include orange liqueur, add 2 tablespoons in step 1 with the orange juice.

Pink lemonade parfaits

KID-FRIENDLY | PREP + COOK TIME **15 MINUTES + COOLING** | SERVES **4**

Fruit parfaits are a popular and easy dessert, especially in summer when the fresh fruit is so sweet and delicious. These strawberry parfaits are topped with Persian cotton candy (pashmak), with its fine filaments of pulled sugar; regular cotton candy may be substituted.

8 oz (225g) strawberries, hulled

$1/3$ cup (80ml) lemonade

$1^1/4$ cups (300ml) whipping cream

$1/3$ cup (110g) lemon curd

$1/3$ cup (15g) shredded coconut, toasted, plus extra 1 tbsp

2.5 oz (71g) cotton candy (see tip)

1 Thinly slice half the strawberries into rounds; quarter the remaining strawberries. Place the quartered strawberries and lemonade in a small pan over high heat; bring to a boil. Reduce the heat; simmer for 5 minutes, mashing the strawberries with a fork a few times during cooking, or until the strawberries soften slightly and the liquid thickens slightly. Allow to cool.

2 Meanwhile, beat the cream in a small bowl using an electric mixer until soft peaks form. Fold the lemon curd and shredded coconut into the whipped cream. Spoon three-quarters of the strawberry mixture onto the cream mixture; do not stir.

3 Spoon the cream mixture into four $2/3$ cup (160ml) glasses. Top with the remaining strawberry mixture, reserved sliced strawberries, cotton candy, and extra coconut.

TIP

If you can't find pashmak or cotton candy, simply sprinkle colored sugar on top instead.

Toffee cannoli

KID-FRIENDLY | PREP + COOK TIME **15 MINUTES** | SERVES **6**

Beloved Sicilian pastries, cannoli are one of those sweet treats where it's difficult to limit yourself to just one. For a more traditional filling, process 5 oz (150g) ricotta cheese until smooth. Whip ½ cup heavy cream to soft peaks; fold the cream and ricotta through the toffee.

1¼ cups (300ml) whipping cream

2 tsp pure vanilla extract

7 oz (200g) chocolate-coated toffee candy, finely chopped, divided

12 store-bought cannoli shells (150g)

sifted powdered sugar, to dust

chocolate ganache

1¼ cup (300ml) whipping cream

3.5 oz (100g) dark chocolate (at least 70% cocoa), coarsely chopped

1 To make the chocolate sauce, heat the cream in a small saucepan until almost boiling, being careful not to scorch; remove from the heat. Add the chocolate; whisk until smooth.

2 In another bowl, beat together the cream and vanilla in a small bowl using an electric mixer until firm peaks form; stir in 5 oz (150g) of the toffee candy.

3 Fit a large piping bag with a large plain nozzle; fill with the toffee cream. Pipe the filling into the cannoli shells; dust with the sifted powdered sugar. Serve the cannoli with the chocolate sauce and remaining brittle.

TIPS

- Chocolate-covered toffee candy is available at major grocery stores.
- If you don't have a piping bag, simply use a zip-top bag; fill the bag with the cream mixture, twist, and snip a ¼ in hole from one corner.
- If you can't find cannoli shells, you could use brandy snap shells instead.

Banana pancakes with chocolate sauce

KID-FRIENDLY | PREP + COOK TIME **30 MINUTES** | SERVES **4**

Bananas and chocolate: a match made in heaven—for chocolate lovers at least. But if bananas aren't your thing in this part of the equation, you can swap them out for another fruit by using the same weight of fresh or frozen cherries or raspberries instead.

1$1/2$ cups (150g) all-purpose flour

1 tsp baking soda

1 tsp baking powder

$1/2$ tsp salt

2 tbsp sugar

1$1/4$ cups (310ml) buttermilk

1 egg, lightly beaten

2 tsp pure maple syrup

2 tbsp (30g) butter, melted and cooled

1 banana (200g), thinly sliced

$1/2$ cup (125ml) whipping cream

2 x 60g chocolate-covered caramel peanut candy bars, coarsely chopped

2 cups (500ml) chocolate ice cream

1 Sift the flour into a large bowl; stir in the baking powder, baking soda, salt, and sugar. Whisk in the combined buttermilk, egg, maple syrup, and butter until the batter is smooth. Stir in the banana.

2 Heat a large oiled skillet over medium heat. Pour $1/4$ cup of the batter into the pan, allowing room for spreading. (You should be able to fit more than 1 pancake in the pan at a time.) Cook for 2 minutes or until bubbles appear on the surface of the pancakes. Turn the pancakes over; cook for 2 minutes or until browned. Remove from the pan; cover to keep warm. Repeat with the remaining batter to make a total of 8 pancakes.

3 Meanwhile, heat the cream in a small saucepan over low heat, add the Snickers bars; stir until melted.

4 Serve the banana pancakes topped with scoops of the chocolate ice cream and the chocolate bar sauce.

Lemon and meringue passionfruit mess

GLUTEN-FREE | PREP + COOK TIME **15 MINUTES** | SERVES **8**

A "mess" is a great way to serve a dessert on a large platter. Guests can serve themselves with as much as they like. The crunchy cookies, tangy lemon curd, and creamy yogurt make a fun dessert that's light after a heavy meal. Make it with fresh or frozen passionfruit pulp.

1¼ cups (300ml) whipping cream

2 tbsp powdered sugar

1 cup (280g) Greek-style yogurt

4 oz (100g) vanilla meringue cookies, coarsely crushed

⅔ cup (200ml) lemon curd

⅓ cup (80g) passionfruit pulp

⅓ cup (15g) flaked coconut, toasted

5 oz (150g) fresh raspberries

1 Using an electric mixer, beat together the cream and powdered sugar in a small bowl until firm peaks form; gently fold in the yogurt.

2 Arrange half of the crushed meringue cookies over a platter. Spoon the cream mixture over the cookies; drop spoonfuls of the lemon curd over the cream. Using a small knife, swirl the curd through the cream.

3 Top with the remaining crumbled cookies, passionfruit pulp, shredded coconut, and raspberries.

Microwave choc-orange lava cake

ONE-POT/KID-FRIENDLY | PREP + COOK TIME **25 MINUTES** | SERVES **4**

It may seem a paradox, but some cakes produce their own saucy center by pouring a more liquidy mixture over a denser batter. During cooking, the liquid falls through the batter as it cooks, to produce an ooey gooey chocolate lava cake.

4 tbsp (60g) butter, chopped, divided

1 cup (110g) all-purpose flour, sifted

1 tsp baking powder

$\frac{1}{2}$ tsp baking soda

$\frac{1}{2}$ tsp salt

$\frac{1}{3}$ cup (110g) sugar

2 tbsp cocoa powder, plus extra 2 tsp

$\frac{2}{3}$ cup (160ml) milk

$\frac{1}{2}$ tsp pure vanilla extract

1.5 oz (80g) orange chocolate, coarsely chopped (see tip)

$\frac{1}{4}$ cup (55g) firmly packed light brown sugar

1 cup (250ml) boiling water

1   Put 2 tablespoons of the chopped butter in a 6-cup microwave-safe dish. Melt in a microwave oven on HIGH (100%) for 1 minute.

2   Add the sifted flour, baking powder, baking soda, salt, sugar, and the 2 tablespoons cocoa powder to the dish with the milk and pure vanilla extract; whisk until smooth. Stir in the chocolate.

3   In a medium bowl, combine the brown sugar and sifted extra 2 teaspoons cocoa powder; gradually stir in the boiling water. Add the remaining chopped butter; stir until the butter melts. Carefully pour the syrup mixture evenly over the back of a spoon, over the cake batter.

4   Microwave on HIGH (100%) for 10 minutes or until just cooked in the center. Allow to stand for 5 minutes before serving with whipped cream or ice cream.

TIP

Don't wait too long to serve the cake, or all the sauce will soak into the cake before you have a chance to enjoy it.

Coconut rice with mango and raspberries

GLUTEN-FREE | PREP + COOK TIME **15 MINUTES** | SERVES **4**

This is a delectable summery rendition of rice pudding, served cool and with the tropical notes of coconut and mango singing through the creamy rice. The tart raspberries cut through the sweetness of the mango and provide acidic balance.

1¼ cup (300ml) whipping cream

½ cup (125ml) coconut cream

½ cup (80g) powdered sugar

2¼ cups (340g) cooked
medium-grain white rice

1 large mango (600g)

125g raspberries

½ cup (25g) toasted shredded coconut

1   Beat the cream, coconut cream, and sugar in a small bowl with an electric mixer until soft peaks form.

2   Place the rice in a large bowl; fold in the cream mixture. Cover with plastic wrap; refrigerate while preparing the mango.

3   Peel the mango, then slice the cheeks thinly and discard the pit. Add the mango to a food processor and pulse until smooth. Divide the rice mixture and mango purée, in alternate layers, among four 1-cup (250ml) serving glasses; top with the raspberries and coconut.

TIPS

- Substitute papaya or summer berries for the mango, if you like.
- To cook the rice in advance, you will need about ¾ cup uncooked medium-grain white rice for this recipe.

Grilled pineapple with mint syrup

GLUTEN-FREE | PREP + COOK TIME **30 MINUTES** | SERVES **8**

Perfectly simple and perfectly delicious, pineapple takes on an intense sweetness when grilled. Choose a yellow-fleshed pineapple for the best flavor. You could use mango cheeks cut from 4 mangoes instead of the pineapple. Drizzle with passionfruit pulp, if you like.

1/2 cup (110g) sugar

1 1/2 cups (40g) firmly packed mint leaves, plus extra 1/4 cup (5g), to serve

1 cup (50g) unsweetened shredded coconut

1 medium pineapple, cut crosswise into 1/2 in thick slices

4 cups (1 liter) vanilla frozen yogurt

1 Preheat the oven to 350°F.

2 Stir the sugar and 1/2 cup (125ml) water in a small saucepan, over medium heat, for 4 minutes or until the sugar dissolves and the syrup reduces slightly. Transfer to a small stainless-steel bowl; freeze for 15 minutes to chill rapidly.

3 Meanwhile, put the 1 1/2 cups (40g) mint in a heatproof bowl. Cover with boiling water; allow to stand for 10 seconds. Drain, then refresh under cold running water. Squeeze to remove any excess water. Set aside.

4 Place the coconut on a parchment-lined baking sheet; bake, shaking the sheet occasionally, for 3 minutes or until golden. Set aside.

5 Preheat a ridged cast-iron grill pan or barbecue to medium-high heat. Cook the pineapple, in two batches, for 2 minutes on each side or until golden.

6 In a food processor, combine the blanched mint and cooled sugar syrup until finely chopped.

7 Divide the grilled pineapple among 8 plates; top with the frozen yogurt. Drizzle with the mint syrup. Serve sprinkled with the shredded coconut and the extra 1/4 cup (5g) mint leaves.

Cherry hazelnut cake

ONE-POT | PREP + COOK TIME **30 MINUTES + STANDING** | SERVES **8**

Make sure to warn diners that the cherries contain pits. If you like, you could add 1 teaspoon of either finely grated lemon zest or finely grated orange zest when beating the butter and sugar in step 2. Almond meal can also be used in place of hazelnut flour.

11 tbsp (150g) butter, softened, plus extra for greasing

²/₃ cup (150g) sugar

2 eggs

1 tsp pure vanilla extract

¹/₂ cup (75g) all-purpose flour

1¹/₂ cups (180g) hazelnut flour

1 tsp baking powder

¹/₂ tsp salt

5 oz (150g) fresh cherries, stems attached

sifted powdered sugar, to dust

³/₄ cup (180ml) whipping cream

¹/₃ cup (80ml) maple syrup

1 Preheat the oven to 400°F. Butter a 9x9 square baking dish or spray with cooking spray.

2 Using an electric mixer, beat together the butter and sugar in a small bowl until pale and fluffy. Add the eggs and vanilla. Beat until just combined, then add the sifted flour, hazelnut flour, baking powder, and salt. Continue beating on low speed until just combined.

3 Spread the mixture evenly into the prepared cake tin; bake for 10 minutes.

4 Top the cake with the cherries, gently pushing them a quarter of the way into the mixture. Bake the cake for a further 10 minutes or until a skewer inserted into the center comes out clean. Stand the cake in the tin for 3 minutes before turning, top-side up, onto a board. Dust with sifted powdered sugar. Serve the cake warm, drizzled with the cream and maple syrup.

Warm rhubarb and gingerbread trifles

KID-FRIENDLY | PREP + COOK TIME **25 MINUTES** | SERVES **4**

Take advantage of the rhubarb season to make these pretty ruby trifles. Select rhubarb with the reddest stems for the best taste and look, and choose good-quality custard and flavorful cake. Using the best of what's available is key when there are so few elements in a dish.

$3^1/_4$ cups (400g) coarsely chopped rhubarb stems

2 tbsp orange juice

$^1/_4$ cup (55g) sugar

2 cups (500ml) thick vanilla custard or pudding

8 oz (225g) gingerbread or pound cake, chopped (see tip)

$^1/_3$ cup (20g) shredded coconut, toasted

2 tbsp coarsely chopped pistachios

1 Combine the rhubarb, orange juice, and sugar in a medium saucepan; bring to a boil. Reduce the heat; simmer, stirring occasionally, for 3 minutes or until the rhubarb is tender.

2 Meanwhile, heat the custard in a small saucepan over low heat.

3 Divide the cake among 4 heatproof serving glasses. Top with the warm custard, then the rhubarb mixture, toasted coconut, and pistachios. Serve immediately.

TIPS

- If you can't find gingerbread pound cake for this recipe, choose another fresh, premade pound cake from the bakery section of your grocery store. Lemon or vanilla would be a nice addition.
- You can also use crushed gingerbread cookies or broken Biscoff cookies instead of the cake.

Passionfruit, lemon, and coconut tarts

GLUTEN-FREE | PREP + COOK TIME **30 MINUTES + COOLING** | MAKES **12**

The shells for these tarts are simple to make and a coconut delight to eat.
If passionfruit isn't available, you can top the coconut tarts with thinly sliced mango
or raspberries. You can find lemon curd in specialty or international grocery stores.

a little butter for greasing

1 cup (90g) unsweetened, shredded coconut

1 egg white, lightly beaten

2 tbsp sugar

2 tbsp whipping cream

$1/2$ cup (160g) lemon curd

2 tbsp passionfruit pulp

1 Preheat the oven to 300°F. Butter 12 holes of a mini muffin tin.

2 In a bowl, combine the coconut, egg white, and sugar in a medium bowl. Press the mixture firmly and evenly over the bottoms and sides of the tin holes. Bake the tart shells for 20 minutes or until lightly browned. Allow to cool; carefully remove from the pan.

3 Meanwhile, beat the cream in a small bowl using an electric mixer until soft peaks form. Gently fold the lemon curd into the cream.

4 Divide the lemon mixture among the coconut cases. Top each tart with a little of the passionfruit pulp.

Dutch baby chocolate pancake with banana

KID-FRIENDLY | PREP + COOK TIME **25 MINUTES** | SERVES **4**

This triple-chocolate dessert is a breeze to make. Just make sure everyone knows that it's meant to be shared! Dutch baby pancakes are made as single large pancakes and baked in the oven, and the Dutch-process cocoa used here is mellower and darker than natural cocoa.

³/₄ cup (180ml) milk

³/₄ cup (100g) all-purpose flour

4 eggs

2 tbsp Dutch-process cocoa powder, plus extra 1 tsp, sifted

¹/₂ cup (110g) sugar

1 tsp pure vanilla extract

3.5 oz (100g) dark chocolate (at least 70% cocoa), coarsely chopped

2 tbsp (30g) butter

¹/₂ lb (250g) bananas, sliced

4 scoops of chocolate or chocolate chip ice cream

1 Preheat the oven to 400°F. At the same time, preheat an 8-inch cast-iron or ovenproof skillet.

2 In a food processor, combine the milk, flour, eggs, the 2 tablespoons cocoa powder, sugar, pure vanilla extract, and a pinch of salt for 15 seconds or until just combined (do not overprocess or the mixture will be tough). Stir in half of the chopped chocolate.

3 Melt the butter in the preheated skillet for 1 minute or until foaming. Add the pancake batter. Immediately transfer to the oven; bake for 12 minutes or until puffed and cooked through.

4 Gently melt the remaining chocolate in a microwave or a small heatproof bowl over a saucepan of simmering water.

5 Top the pancake with the bananas and ice cream, drizzle with the melted chocolate, and dust with the extra 2 teaspoons sifted cocoa powder. Serve the pancake immediately.

TIP

Dutch-process cocoa powder is darker than natural cocoa powder and has a mellower flavor. It goes through an alkalizing process when it is made, neutralizing the natural acidity of the cocoa beans.

Spiced rhubarb and strawberry crumbles

KID-FRIENDLY | PREP + COOK TIME **25 MINUTES + COOLING** | SERVES **4**

Fruit crumbles are often seen as a comfort food for a wintry night, but this one makes the most of summer's seasonal bounty. The crumble mixture can be made a day ahead; store in an airtight container until needed. You can also serve it as a topping for other desserts.

a little butter for greasing

1/4 cup (60ml) maple syrup

1 1/4 lb (100g) shortbread cookies, coarsely chopped

4 oz (125g) macadamia nuts, coarsely chopped

3/4 lb (400g) rhubarb, trimmed (any leaves discarded), cut into 2 in pieces

8 oz (225g) strawberries, quartered

1 tsp pure vanilla extract

1/4 cup (55g) sugar

1 tsp ground ginger

1/2 tsp ground cinnamon

1 Preheat the oven to 400°F. Line a large baking sheet with parchment paper.

2 In a medium bowl, combine the maple syrup, shortbread, and macadamias; spread out on the prepared baking sheet. Bake in the oven for 4 minutes; stir, then bake for a further 4 minutes or until golden. Allow to cool.

3 Meanwhile, put the rhubarb, strawberries, pure vanilla extract, sugar, and spices in a medium saucepan over medium heat; cook, stirring, for 3 minutes or until the juices run from the fruit. Continue cooking, stirring occasionally, for a further 5 minutes or until the rhubarb has softened but still holds its shape.

4 Divide the fruit mixture among 4 small bowls; top with the crumble mixture to serve.

TIP

You could also make the crumble mixture with your favorite cookies; however, keep in mind that it is best to choose a buttery, un-iced variety.

Watermelon, lime, and berry cheesecake jars

KID-FRIENDLY | PREP + COOK TIME **15 MINUTES** | SERVES **4**

This superfast deconstructed cheesecake can be assembled and served in glasses or serving bowls instead of jars, if you like. Delving with your spoon through the layers of summer fruit and creamy cheese to find the gingery crumbs below becomes part of the joy of eating.

½ lb (400g) gingersnaps

3 tbsp (50g) butter

1 lime (90g)

8 oz (225g) mascarpone cheese

8 oz (225g) cream cheese

⅓ cup (55g) powdered sugar, sifted, plus extra 2 tsp

¼ lb (125g) raspberries

¼ lb (125g) seedless watermelon, diced into 1cm pieces

1 tbsp finely shredded mint

1 In the bowl of a food processor, pulse the gingersnaps until finely chopped. Add the butter; pulse until just combined. Divide the crumb mixture evenly among four 1½-cup (375ml) jars.

2 Finely grate the zest of the lime, then juice (you will need 2 tablespoons of lime juice). In the food processor, combine the lime zest and juice, mascarpone cheese, cream cheese, and sifted powdered sugar until smooth. Divide the cheese mixture evenly among the jars; tap gently on a work surface to level the mixture.

3 Put the raspberries and extra 2 teaspoons powdered sugar in a bowl. Using the back of a fork, lightly crush the berries, stirring until the powdered sugar dissolves. Stir in the watermelon.

4 Divide the watermelon mixture evenly among the jars; top each one with the mint to serve.

Chocolate dulce de leche cakes

KID-FRIENDLY | PREP + COOK TIME **30 MINUTES** | SERVES **4**

Dulce de leche is a Latin American caramel made by reducing milk and sugar until it is a gloriously thick, dark caramel. It can be used as a spread or topping for everything from cakes to ice cream, and has infinite uses in desserts.

$1/3$ cup (120g) dulce de leche, divided

$3/4$ cup (165g) sugar

7 tbsp (100g) butter, melted, cooled, plus extra for greasing

$1/3$ cup (100g) all-purpose flour, sifted

$1/2$ tsp baking powder

$1/2$ tsp salt

2 tbsp almond meal or crushed almonds

$1/3$ cup (35g) Dutch-process cocoa powder, sifted, plus extra $1/2$ tsp, to dust

$1/3$ cup (80ml) milk

2 eggs

1 tsp pure vanilla extract

1.75 oz (50g) dark chocolate (at least 70% cocoa), finely chopped

$1/2$ cup (110g) firmly packed brown sugar

1 cup (250ml) boiling water

4 small scoops of vanilla ice cream

1 Preheat the oven to 400°F. Grease six 1-cup or four $1^{1}/3$ cups ovenproof ramekins with a little butter. Place on a baking sheet lined with parchment paper.

2 Meanwhile, spoon 1 tablespoon of the dulce de leche into the bottom of each dish.

3 In the food processor, combine the sugar, melted butter, flour, baking powder, salt, ground almonds, 2 tablespoons of the sifted cocoa powder, milk, eggs, and pure vanilla extract. Process until smooth. Transfer the mixture to a large bowl; stir in the chopped chocolate. Spoon the mixture evenly into the prepared ramekins.

4 Combine the brown sugar and remaining cocoa powder into a small bowl; sprinkle the sugar mixture evenly over cakes. Holding a spoon with the back facing upward over each cake, carefully pour 3-4 tablespoons boiling water over the surface of each one to wet the sugar mixture completely.

5 Bake the cakes for 25 minutes or until the top is cakelike and firm to the touch. Dust with the extra $1/2$ teaspoon sifted cocoa powder. Serve immediately, topped with the ice cream and accompanied by extra dulce de leche, if you like.

TIP

Dulce de leche is available in cans in the baking section of your grocery store. (Look for it by the evaporated and sweetened condensed milk.)

Conversion chart

A note on Australian measures

- One Australian metric measuring cup holds approximately 250ml.

- One Australian metric tablespoon holds 20ml.

- One Australian metric teaspoon holds 5ml.

- The difference between one country's measuring cups and another's is within a two- or three-teaspoon variance, and should not affect your cooking results.

- North America, New Zealand, and the United Kingdom use a 15ml tablespoon.

Using measures in this book

- All cup and spoon measurements are level.

- The most accurate way of measuring dry ingredients is to weigh them.

- When measuring liquids, use a clear glass or plastic jug with metric markings.

- We use large eggs with an average weight of 60g.

Dry measures

metric	imperial
15g	$1/2$oz
30g	1oz
60g	2oz
90g	3oz
125g	4oz ($1/4$lb)
155g	5oz
185g	6oz
220g	7oz
250g	8oz ($1/2$lb)
280g	9oz
315g	10oz
345g	11oz
375g	12oz ($3/4$lb)
410g	13oz
440g	14oz
470g	15oz
500g	16oz (1lb)
750g	24oz ($1 1/2$lb)
1kg	32oz (2lb)

Liquid measures

metric	imperial
30ml	1 fluid oz
60ml	2 fluid oz
100ml	3 fluid oz
125ml	4 fluid oz
150ml	5 fluid oz
190ml	6 fluid oz
250ml	8 fluid oz
300ml	10 fluid oz
500ml	16 fluid oz
600ml	20 fluid oz
1000ml (1 liter)	$1 3/4$ pints

Length measures

metric	imperial
3mm	$1/8$in
6mm	$1/4$in
1cm	$1/2$in
2cm	$3/4$in
2.5cm	1in
5cm	2in
6cm	$2 1/2$in
8cm	3in
10cm	4in
13cm	5in
15cm	6in
18cm	7in
20cm	8in
22cm	9in
25cm	10in
28cm	11in
30cm	12in (1ft)

Oven temperatures

The oven temperatures in this book are for conventional ovens; if you have a fan-forced oven, decrease the temperature by 10–20 degrees.

	°C (Celsius)	°F (Fahrenheit)
Very slow	120	250
Slow	150	300
Moderately slow	160	325
Moderate	180	350
Moderately hot	200	400
Hot	220	425
Very hot	240	475

Index

Acknowledgments

DK would like to thank Sophia Young, Joe Reville, Amanda Chebatte, and Georgia Moore for their assistance in making this book.

The Australian Women's Weekly Test Kitchen in Sydney has developed, tested, and photographed the recipes in this book.